How to Write
POLICIES
PROCEDURES and
TASK OUTLINES

Third Edition

by Larry Peabody

How to Write Policies, Procedures, and Task Outlines

First Edition Copyright © 1983 by Larry Peabody

Second Edition Copyright © 1996 by Larry Peabody

Third Edition Copyright © 2001, 2006, and 2010 by Larry Peabody

ISBN 978-0-9650585-0-6

Published by WRITING SERVICES, 7509 Magnolia Ct. S.E., Lacey, WA   98503

CONTENTS

Foreword .... **v**

Chapter 1   Introduction 1

Chapter 2   Diagnosis..**11**
　　　　　　Writing Style 11
　　　　　　Page Layout 15
　　　　　　Organization 17

Chapter 3   Definitions **23**
　　　　　　Policy.. 24
　　　　　　Procedure.. 24
　　　　　　Task Outline 26

Chapter 4   Policies **31**
　　　　　　Part One: Planning a Policy 31
　　　　　　Part Two: Writing a Policy 37

Chapter 5   Procedures **55**
　　　　　　Part One: Planning a Procedure 55
　　　　　　Part Two: Writing a Procedure 69

Chapter 6   Task Outlines **85**

Chapter 7   Numbering System **93**

Chapter 8   Manual Management..............................**103**
　　　　　　Getting the Most out of Your System.......... 103
　　　　　　Whether and What to Write 107

Appendixes Writer's Kit **109**

　　　　　　Index .... **.117**

FOREWORD

In the first edition of this manual, I wrote the following foreword:

About a month after a recent workshop on methods for writing guidance, I reconvened the class and asked them to look over what all the others had written after the training. Most participants did a splendid job of using the new formats. But one person had lapsed back into typical writing style. Class reaction was swift and certain: the new formats had "spoiled" them. They had no patience whatsoever for reading something written the old way.

This book offers the same methods I present in my policy-procedure-task writing workshops. Because this is a how-to book, it's filled with examples that show principles at work in specific contexts. All the examples come from criminal justice agencies. You may or may not work in that field--which leads me to add two comments.

If you do work in the criminal justice system, I'll ask you not to view the examples as models you can use intact. Concentrate on the writing techniques, not on the content of the examples. Although they came from existing manuals, the examples may not exactly fit the situation in your state, county, city, or agency.

If, on the other hand, you work in some business or public agency that is not a part of the criminal justice system, don't let the examples stop you just because they're "foreign." Once you've grasped the concepts, the formats and worksheets (Writer's Kit) will work just as well with your own material.

Much has changed since then, but that foreword has held up pretty well. I think that's because the main points in this book--the definitions of policies, procedures, and task outlines and the formats for writing them--have held up so well. Hundreds of students from many kinds of organizations have learned to use these methods. Their response has been overwhelmingly favorable. So whether you are in a business, public agency, or nonprofit organization, I'm confident this book can help you.

The Second Edition

The Second Edition of this book recognized and adjusted for some advances in technology. When this book was first prepared, typewriters still outnumbered computers in most offices. By 1996, nearly all organizations were using word processors or desktop publishing programs.

Computers have opened up whole new possibilities in issuing written direction.

Today, some organizations are doing away with policy and procedure *manuals* entirely. They're putting their written direction "online," using the local computer network. These "virtual manuals," with their advantages and disadvantages, are likely to become increasingly common.

Other large organizations with far-flung operations have begun issuing policy and procedure manuals on computer disks. These make policies, procedures, and forms instantly available almost anywhere.

Why a Third Edition?

Most changes driven by the computer revolution don't affect the content of this book. But the increasing use of online manuals requires a whole new way of approaching the numbering system—the topic of chapter seven. This third edition includes a numbering system developed especially for online use. It permits you to assign numbers that may be used as filenames and as HTML hot links for cross-referencing.

Neither revision has turned this into a computer book. It's still aimed squarely at the writing process, which has the same goal whether you distribute the finished product on paper or on screen. That goal will always be *to reproduce the writer's ideas in the reader's mind.* I hope this book will help you close in on that target.

—Larry Peabody—

Chapter One:

INTRODUCTION

Are Readable Policies and Procedures Possible?

Imagine you have just joined the staff of a county jail. Shortly after you've located the coffee pot and the rest room, someone hands you a manual entitled Standard Operating Procedures. Here, you hope, you'll learn how to function in your new role. But what's this?

The Jail Supervisor shall be the classification officer. If he is not present at the time the prisoner is booked, the jailer on duty will act on behalf of the supervisor. Although the final determination as to classification is a responsibility of the Jail Supervisor. The determination will be made by the Jail Supervisor and assisted by any observations or knowledge the booking officer may have in regards to the prisoner. In the absence of the Jail Supervisor, the Sheriff shall act as the classification officer unless another staff member has been appointed in writing by the Jail Supervisor.

Although the intended thought got garbled, another message comes through clearly: "Don't bother to try to read this stuff. Ask around. Learn what you need to know by word-of-mouth." Every day policy-procedure manuals in thousands of companies and agencies send the same between-the-lines message to employees. Little wonder that readers resist reading written directions.

As an experiment, I once asked eight members of a writing workshop to role-play their way through the following procedure from a state prison manual. Each of the eight received a card naming the part he or she would play. The "cast of characters" included: the Correctional Supervisor; the Classification and Parole Supervisor; the Living Unit; the Administrative Lieutenant; the Administrative Segregation Hearing Committee; the Unit Team; and the Inmate.

Each also received a copy of this procedure:

REMOVING AN INMATE FROM ADMINISTRATIVE SEGREGATION

A. When an inmate's Unit Team makes a determination that a man should be returned from Administrative Segregation to his living unit, he is to notify the Classification and Parole Supervisor and **coordinate with him, since he arranges for all room moves throughout the Training Center.**

B. If the Administrative Segregation Hearing Committee makes a recommendation that an inmate is to be returned to his original living unit, the Correctional Unit Supervisor and the Unit Team are not mandated to take the inmate back. Discussion should take place between the Correctional Unit Supervisor and the Administrative Lieutenant regarding the recommended move, but the final decision to move an inmate out of Administrative Segregation belongs to the Unit Team.

C. If arrangements are made by unit staff for an inmate to transfer to another facility, the inmate will transfer directly from Administrative Segregation to that facility.

The results weren't surprising. The eight "players" had no clue how to proceed. They argued a bit, did some foot-shuffling, then gave up. No one was sure who should take the first step or exactly what that first step might be.

In businesses and public agencies, that same confusion created by poorly written direction costs more than anyone has ever calculated. Hours and dollars waste away when employees:

1. Spend more time reading than doing.

2. Understand slowly—and miss deadlines.

3. Pick up the wrong idea, so take incorrect action.

4. Draw a blank and do nothing.

And those are just the *reading* costs. The cost of *writing* the directions in the first place adds even more to the waste.

No one knew who should take the first step or what that first step might be.

In *The New Playscript Procedure,* Leslie H. Matthies says it takes from 8 to 12 days' work to draft and issue a single procedure—roughly two weeks. If he's right, you don't need a calculator to estimate the writing costs. And if no one can follow the directions after they're on paper, all those dollars will buy nothing but obstacles to productivity.

What's the answer?

• *Write Nothing?* You might decide to do away with written directions. Let everyone learn what to do by trial and error. Tempting, perhaps, but hardly practical. Without written directions you leave yourself open to all the distortions of the old gossip game. Beyond that, your organization may be legally required to spell out your policies and procedures on paper.

• *Hire a Writing Pro?* You might choose to hire professional writers. After six months or a year, they would probably produce a manual even newcomers could follow. But outside writers insist on being paid. Two or three staff members would have to teach them all about your operation. Then, after you'd invested all this time and money, the manual would soon go out of date. So you would have to bring the professionals back—and back up to speed—again and again.

If you want something done right . . .

• *Write It Yourselves?* But there's a third answer. You and your co-workers can draft written directions anyone can follow easily. You don't have to be professional writers. You need only three qualifications:

1. Know your agency and how it should work.

2. Have a working grasp of the English language. (No need for you to become gurus in grammar.)

3. Learn how to tell policy, procedure, and task apart and how to select and use the best format for each.

You almost certainly qualify on the first two counts. And you can quickly develop skill in the third area by working through the definitions and examples in this book. Even if you barely survived high-school writing classes, you can learn to write effective policies, procedures and task outlines. They may not win any literary prizes. But they'll do what you send them out to do—to direct the actions of those overworked people who make your organization produce.

You may suspect that last statement. Is it just hype? Here you are—with too much to read already—at the beginning of a book that asks you to invest several hours in studying some new methods. You're probably asking yourself, "Is this book worth my time? Will it really show me how to write policies and procedures that work better than the ones we have now?"

For a dramatic picture of the difference the methods in this book can make, compare pages 5 and 6 with pages 7, 8, and 9.

The examples that follow may help you answer those questions. The first piece is from an actual policy and procedure manual. After it come three shorter pieces that illustrate how the original directions might have appeared had they been written with the methods you'll learn in this book. Read each piece thoroughly—then ask yourself which version you and your co-workers would be more likely to read, grasp on the run, and follow.

The original piece appears as written in a typical policy and procedure manual.

TRANSPORTING PERSONS IN CUSTODY

Wordy - nd.
Can't find.
key points.

General

The transportation of probation and parole violators is a normal probation and parole officer function. As a general rule, the extradition and return of a parole violator from another state is handled by the division, while the return of a probation violator is a responsibility of the county of conviction. Probationers are more frequently transported for short distances within the state. County authorities should be encouraged to accept this responsibility. If they do not, the Probation and Parole Division may transport probationers.

The transporting of a violator from another state is coordinated by the deputy compact administrator in headquarters. While most out-of-state prisoner transports are handled by the transportation officer located in the headquarters office, probation and parole officers occasionally make these trips when the transportation officer is unable to do so. The probation and parole officer to be assigned to transport is selected by a supervisor, with the officer who is supervising the case given the first consideration. Workload factors and officer preference are considered. For potentially hazardous transports, a staff member with sufficient experience and physical strength is selected. Written instructions (see example 720.587) and other necessary documents are provided to the officer by the deputy compact administrator.

Prisoners who are being returned are frequently anxious and concerned about their situation. It is natural that the conversation between the prisoner and the officer turns to this subject. The officer should avoid offering judgments, opinions, or predictions of what may happen to the prisoner. Admonishing, arguing, or talking to the prisoner in a way that might evoke antagonism is to be avoided. It is important that conversation be as pleasant and relaxed as possible to keep from increasing the prisoner's anxiety.

While there are general guidelines governing transporting prisoners, there are too many variables for them to cover all situations. Good organization and appropriate planning of the transport will reduce the frequency and lessen the difficulty of dealing with unanticipated developments. A fundamental precept is to obtain assistance as soon as a need to do so is apparent. The deputy compact administrator in headquarters may be called at any time for advice. A transporting officer should not be hesitant in placing a prisoner in a detention facility and/or restraints when time is needed to resolve a problem, or when the security of the prisoner or other persons is the least bit questionable.

Use of restraints is mandatory during all phases of the transport except in detention cells, and in court rooms and aircraft where restraints are not permitted. In the event the use of restraints aboard an aircraft is deemed necessary, this is to be cleared with the captain. The usual restraints used for transporting are handcuffs and "belly chains" or "waistraints."

Legal Authority to Transport

It is essential that officers have formal material to assure the transfer of custody of prisoners for transporting purposes and for subsequent use in booking prisoners into other facilities. The officer must have official agency identification and a warrant or an order authorizing detention which is acceptable to a receiving facility. For cases being returned from other states, additional material includes a formal warrant and extradition papers or a waiver of extradition. On occasion a transport will be arranged without the signed waiver in hand. This is sometimes done in the interest of time when a teletype message is received from the detaining agency stating that the individual has signed a waiver of extradition. In this event the officer will be instructed to pick up copies of the signed waiver in the other state.

There are three general types of legal means by which a person is transported between states: 1) cases where extradition is not an issue; 2) cases formally extradited; and 3) cases where extradition has been legally waived. Every person scheduled for return to this state in custody has a right through legal means to resist being returned. If that right is not waived, extradition procedures are initiated. If extradition is allowed, the person is returned over his or her objection.

There are two ways that extradition may be waived. Either the person must have signed a waiver of extradition prior to leaving the state or voluntarily sign new waivers at the time return is requested. The waivers signed prior to the person leaving the state are processed through the procedures of the Interstate Compact for the Supervision of Probationers and Parolees. Extradition papers, the Rendition Warrant, or the waivers of extradition usually have been processed by the Interstate Compact authorities prior to a transporting officer becoming involved, with appropriate copies provided to the officer along with other documents. While a prisoner may have waived extradition or may be extradited, a court appearance may be a routine formality or may be necessary to resolve some point. Occasionally, courts are not familiar with their own state's Interstate Compact laws. If it appears that a problem is developing in the other state, this should be reported to the appropriate deputy compact administrator in the headquarters office immediately by telephone.

(The next three pages present the same subject written in the style this book will present and explain.)

Effective Date:	**POLICY**	**Page: of**
Cancels:		
See Also:		**Approved by:** _____

POL-321 TRANSPORTING PROBATION AND PAROLE VIOLATORS

This policy applies whenever any officer is assigned to transport a person in custody, either in state or across state lines.

1. Deputy Compact Administrator Coordinates All Transports

The Deputy Compact Administrator (DCA) in headquarters will
- Schedule all transports.
- Obtain any legal documents required to authorize the transport.
- Provide written instructions for the transporting officer to use.

2. State Transportation Officers Usually Conduct Out-of-State Transports *

When interstate travel is required, the DCA will usually assign a state transportation officer to accompany the prisoner. However, the DCA may assign a Probation and Parole Officer (PPO) to an interstate transport.

3. County Authorities Should Conduct In-State Transports

The DCA will urge county officials to transport probation violators between counties within this state. If a county official refuses to transport a prisoner within the state, the DCA may assign a state PPO to the task.

4. Restraints Are Required Throughout All Transports

The transporting officer must always restrain prisoners (with handcuffs, "belly chains," or "waistraints") during transports, except
- In detention cells.
- In courtrooms.
- On aircraft when airline rules prohibit them.

* *paragraph revised*

Effective Date:	**PROCEDURE**	**Page: of**
Cancels: **See Also:**		**Approved by:** _____

PRO-321A <u>TRANSPORTING PROBATION AND PAROLE VIOLATORS</u>

<u>Action by:</u>   <u>Action:</u>

Deputy Compact
Administrator

1. **Receives** notice from the Parole Board to transport a probation or parole violator.

2. **Obtains** legal authority to move the prisoner (TSK-321B).

3. **Sends** written instructions and any required legal forms to the responsible supervisor.

Supervisor

4. **Assigns** a Transporting Officer (or Probation and Parole Officer) to transport the prisoner.

    4a. If the prisoner is likely to be violent, **assigns** an experienced, physically strong officer.

5. **Gives** the transporting officer the written instructions and any legal forms required.

Transporting Officer

6. **Transports** the prisoner as directed (TSK-321A).

Effective Date:		Page: of
	TASK OUTLINE	
Cancels:		
See Also:		**Approved by:** _____

TSK-321A <u>TRANSPORTING PROBATION AND PAROLE VIOLATORS</u>

After being assigned by the supervisor to transport a prisoner, the
<u>Transporting Officer:</u>

1. **Gets** written instructions and any legally required documents from
the Supervisor.

2. **Reviews** instructions.

3. **Plans** the transport carefully to anticipate and avoid difficulties.

4. **Arranges** own travel to the prisoner pickup point.

5. **Presents** legal documents for out-of-state officials to obtain custody
of prisoner.

6. If legal complications or potential security problems arise:

    6a. **May place** the prisoner in a detention facility or in restraints.

    6b. **May telephone** the Deputy Compact Administrator for advice or
    assistance.

7. **Uses** restraints at all times during transport (POL-321).

8. **Avoids** discussing with the prisoner the possible outcome of the case.

9. **Keeps** conversation with the prisoner as pleasant and relaxed as
possible to avoid increasing the prisoner's anxiety.

10. **Delivers** the prisoner to the prearranged destination.

11. **Files** report of transport with the Deputy Compact Administrator.

(This Page for Notes)

Chapter Two:

DIAGNOSIS

Why do so many policies and procedures fail?

I have led hundreds of writing workshops, many of them for people working in correctional agencies. Before class I often study writing samples from those who will attend. Time after time, I find the same dozen writing pitfalls that ruin policies and procedures. Just avoid this "deadly dozen," and your writing will easily outperform most of what other organizations grind out. The dozen pitfalls fit into three major groups: *Writing Style, Page Layout, and Organization.*

WRITING STYLE: HEAVY, PASSIVE, VAGUE

1. Sentences Run Too Long

Want to *put off* readers? It's easy. Just use sentences that average 30 or 35 words long. One survey found that two-thirds of the readers had trouble following material that averaged 33 words per sentence.

Here's an example from a court procedure. Maybe the writer didn't know long sentences stop readers cold:

Two 16-word sentences let readers grasp more than a single 32-word sentence.

When an alleged violator makes an appointment for a hearing and subsequently fails to appear for that appointment or makes no attempt to reestablish a new hearing date on the next day or (whenever the dockets are received) a default penalty of $25.00 is added and the Department of Licensing is notified. (52 words)

Even several re-readings won't help most readers get the point. The two appearances of "or" make the sentence twist like a stunt plane. Here's another way to write the same thing:

If a citizen misses a hearing without first trying to reschedule it, charge a $25 default fine. Notify the

Licensing Department on the next day or as soon as the dockets arrive. (32 words, 16 words average per sentence)

Which of the two versions is more likely to be understood?

2. <u>Long Words Clog the Flow of Ideas</u>

This is from the introduction to a policy statement:

Conduct within the rules and regulations of the corrections facility is requisite to the safe, secure operation of the facility as well as the effective implementation and administration of inmate discipline.

Of the 31 words in that sentence, 10 bulge with three syllables or more. Notwithstanding, the unanimous conclusion of readability researchers affirms that excessive utilization of polysyllabic terminology introduces a reduction in comprehension. (Translation: Reading experts agree—too many long words hide the meaning.)

Overuse of long words—like overuse of long sentences—will cause many readers to miss your point. A few long words don't add much difficulty, if the reader knows them. But when nearly one word in three comes in jumbo size, many readers will fail to follow your thought.

Now try reading the same introductory statement rewritten in mostly one- and two-syllable words—with just one "long" word in the bunch:

We will use disciplinary action to enforce jail rules and to promote greater safety for inmates, jail staff, and the public.

Which of the two—the original or the revision—left a clearer idea in your mind? Which would you rather read?

3. <u>Subheadings Merely Label—They Say Nothing</u>

Effective writing uses headlines to give readers the essence of what they're about to read. These "advance organizers" prepare the reader to enter the unfamiliar "turf"

Words offer shortcuts to understanding. Short words make the best shortcuts.

of ideas that lie ahead. But in many policy statements, the subheadings don't predict much of anything. For example:

Restrictions

No individual shall be on the approved visiting list of more than one inmate at the same time. The only exceptions will be for family members visiting family members at this institution, i.e., parents may visit at the same time with, or be on the approved visiting list for, two sons incarcerated at the institution.

A headline gives away the main point up front.

That subheading, *Restrictions*, merely labels the subject of the paragraph without hinting what those restrictions might be. To find out, the reader must dig into the paragraph itself. But suppose the reader—before reading the paragraph—had come across a headline that gave away the main point up front. Like this:

Visitors May Normally Visit Only One Inmate

These seven words flag the key idea of the section. This helps readers grasp the more detailed statement that will follow. Here are some other examples of terse, label subheadings followed by revisions that show the more useful summary headlines:

(Label) **Authority of Duty Officer**

(Summary) **Duty Officer Controls Non-Standard Shifts**

(Label) **Review of Denial**

(Summary) **Superintendent Reviews all Requests for Denial**

Don't try to write headlines that are 100 percent complete down to the smallest detail. The subheading does not replace the paragraph. It merely helps the reader get into the paragraph with fair warning of what's coming.

4. Lifeless Verbs Add Length and Prompt Yawns

After working a few years, many of us pick up the passive writing virus. And no wonder. Most of what we read at

Active verbs cut length and keep readers awake.

work exposes us to sickly subjects and verbs. Passive writing requires 20 to 30 percent more words than active writing to express the same ideas. Worse, passive writing bores readers—one reason so few people bother reading policies and procedures.

This 44-word clunker comes from a procedure on writing a presentence report:

It is emphasized, however, that despite the officer's freedom to choose what is to be included in the personal history section, a thorough investigation concerning *all* subsections is necessary before a choice can be made as to what information should be included or omitted.

You can deliver those ideas in fewer words with active subjects and verbs. Here's a 28-word revision:

Officers may choose what to write in the personal history section. But they must consider all subsections before deciding what to include in or omit from that section.

The revision is two-thirds as long and easier to understand. Which would you read when rushed?

5. Many Doers Disappear

When passive verbs let doers disappear, readers won't know who's responsible.

Passive writing isn't just dull. It often lets those responsible for the action—the "doers"— disappear. It's possible (and grammatically permissible) to write an English sentence without a doer, because passive verbs let the "doees" serve as subjects.

That's a problem when the reader scans written directions. Policies and procedures—especially procedures—should say *who* does what. If the doer drops out of sight, the reader must guess—as in the next example:

The transporting officer will be instructed to pick up copies of the signed waiver of extradition in the other state.

Who instructs the officer? The supervisor? The deputy compact administrator? The superintendent? Because the doer doesn't appear, perhaps no one will do it. But with the doer as the subject of the sentence it's easy for readers to see the answer at once:

The supervisor will instruct the officer to pick up copies of the signed waiver of extradition in the other state.

6. Vague Modifiers Create Unanswered Questions

Examples of vague modifiers:
- **proper**
- **relevant**
- **appropriate**
- **timely**
- **normal**

Readers use policies and procedures to get clear directions. But all too often they find modifiers that raise more questions than they answer. Examples:

If oral surgery is required, the inmate will be transferred to the proper institution for treatment.

The secretary assigns the camp number and enters relevant material on the Population Roster

Duty officers shall keep the superintendent advised in a timely manner of all incidents and decisions outside the normal operation of the institution.

Which institution is "proper"? Does the reader know which data is "relevant"? Does "timely" mean 2 hours or 48? What are "normal" operations?

PAGE LAYOUT: FULL OF FRICTION

7. Pages Cover Too Much

In one policy and procedures manual, a single page covered policies and procedures for these topics:

Closure Procedure Following Probation Revocation

Temporary Placement (Maintenance) Programs

Layover Investigation

Too many topics on one page add "friction" that readers must overcome to get through the material. The sheer volume of material overwhelms the eyes. Instead of helping readers focus their attention on one subject, the page itself distracts them.

Page-cramming creates other problems as well. First, consider the revision that shrinks or expands the piece it replaces. The change in length will disturb the material before and after it. If two policies or procedures had been occupying the same page, one of them will get bumped. Revisions are never much fun—but they're even less so with this ripple effect. Difficult revisions probably won't come out on time, putting the manual behind the times and reducing the chances readers will open and use it.

Including more than one policy on a page complicates the revision-making process.

Second, as we'll discuss later, you can produce individually-tailored manuals to fit each of your readers. But if you crowd more than one policy or procedure on a page, you'll either have to give readers more than they need or give them pages with policies and procedures chopped off in midstream.

 Is leftover white space "wasted"? Not at all. Easy-to-read policies and procedures with generous white space get used—unlike those with too many words shoehorned onto every page.

8. <u>Long Paragraphs Turn Readers Away</u>

If you read many policies and procedures, this probably doesn't require any proof. But consider this brick of text:

Administrative segregation and protective custody inmates shall submit a lay-in to the law library for access. The staff librarian will schedule inmates to the law library Mondays, Wednesdays, Thursdays, and Fridays from 11:30 a.m. to 12:30 p.m. It shall be the responsibility of correctional staff as well as the law librarian to coordinate access to the library. In conjunction with Policy Directive 83.582, it shall be the responsibility of custody officials to determine if inmates housed in BCI, KNS, TDS, SNU, or in transit pose a threat to themselves or to the security of the institution before allowing access to the law library. If it is determined the inmate poses a threat to himself or the security of the institution, he will not be allowed physical access to the law library. The inmate shall

submit a request in writing to the law library indicating what legal materials or supplies he needs to assist himself. Photocopies of legal material shall be made for the inmate by the staff librarian on each Tuesday from 1:00 p.m. to 3:00 p.m. Legal material will be delivered to those inmates on Wednesday of each week by the law librarian.

Long paragraphs look intimidating. That's why so many readers refuse to enter them.

A paragraph that long requires forced entry. The visual and mental effort required to break in takes more energy than readers care to invest. So they won't. They either guess at the procedure, ask someone to tell them what to do, or just ignore the whole thing until a crisis comes along. Then, at the worst moment, the whole organization has to stop to confront and clarify the issue.

A few eye-inviting paragraphs could have made the whole matter clear from the start. But don't expect clarity from such a massive eyesore.

9. Long Lines Add More Friction

Judging from the length of the lines in a typical policy and procedure manual, a reader new to our planet might conclude our paper was rationed. The line-length in many manuals approaches 80 characters wide.

Imagine reading a newspaper with columns a foot wide.

Compare those "wide loads" with the text in newspapers and magazines, which survive by attracting readers. We've come to expect those narrower columns—some barely over 30 characters wide. It all started with some research demonstrating that readers' eyes do best when lines run about one and a half alphabets (39 characters) long.

That's not to say we should lop off every line at 39 characters. But it does suggest we adjust the formats for policies and procedures to reduce long-line friction.

ORGANIZATION: OUT OF KILTER

10. Lists Fall from Parallel Form

Well-organized lists can make reading easier by breaking up a page of heavy print and showing how the items are related. But some lists look like heaps of two-by-fours thrown together, with the ends jutting out in all directions—impossible to grasp easily. Here's one:

In the report, the following information should be provided:

Noun

1. Felony arrests and convictions in chronological order, mentioning date of arrest, place, arresting agency, charge and disposition, if available.

2. If the defendant has served time in an institution, parole date(s), parole status, etc., must be provided.

Verb.

3. Mention all outstanding warrants/detainers, pending charges including arrests after present offense, status of prosecution, and case number.

An out-of-parallel list forces the reader to stop and make adjustments the writer should have made.

Well done lists read as if each item were cut from the same pattern. In the non-parallel example above, each item does its own thing:

- Item one begins with an adjective followed by a noun *(Felony arrests...)*.

- Item two begins with a conditional phrase *(If...)*.

- Item three starts off with a verb *(Mention ...)*.

So while the reader's eye searches for a consistent parallel pattern, there isn't any. Compare that original list with the revision below. In the new list, all three items share the same structure. This helps the reader follow easily.

In the report, the following information should be provided:

1. Felony arrests and convictions in chronological order. (If available, include the date and place of arrest, arresting agency, charge, and disposition.)

2. Parole dates and status (if the defendant has served time in prison).

3. **Outstanding warrants/detainers, pending charges (including any arrests after the present offense), status of prosecution, and case number.**

The predictable pattern of parallel structure lets the reader relax. This last example follows an adjective-noun; adjective-noun; adjective-noun pattern—but that's just one of many possible patterns.

11. Time Tumbles Out of Order

When writing directions, always list the steps in chronological order.

The goal of policies and procedures is to help direct the choices and actions of the people in your organization as they carry out its mission. In other words, helping people "do what needs to be done." A major part of doing what needs to be done is doing things in the right order. But some writers seem to lose their sense of timing when they write procedures.

The procedure on the next page came from a jail manual. Each numbered step appears in its original sequence. The bracketed numbers suggest the order a reader would have to follow to carry out the procedure. The original sequence is so scrambled, some bracketed numbers appear twice.

Escape or Attempted Escape

This section is written to minimize confusion and overreaction during an escape, prevent any other escapes, establish guidelines for use of force, and effect the fast and safe recovery of escapees.

1. Secure the escape exit, and notify the Shift Supervisor with a description of the escapee. *[2] [3]*

    a. Name
    b. Female or male
    c. Race
    d. Age
    e. Clothing description
    f. Personal description
    g. Weapons, if any
    h. Direction of travel and pursuit

2. Obtain a mug shot from County Police or City Police Department ID Bureau to distribute to Officers in searching for escapee. *[6]*

3. The Shift Supervisor orders a general lockdown of all inmates, notifies the County Police Department and the City Police Department, and calls the Jail Commander (or her/his designee) and the Director of the Department of Rehabilitative Services. *[4] [5]*

4. During the period of the lockdown, Deck Officers conduct a name and number count of the entire population to determine the identity of all escapees and to insure that no other escapees are undetected. *[7]*

5. With all available Corrections Officers, begin searching the entire Jail to ascertain the location of the inmates and escapees. Always consider the possibility of a diversionary action by the escaping inmates. Maintain adequate staffing of security posts. *[8]*

6. If an inmate escapes from your personal custody, give pursuit. If you fail in your attempt to recapture the inmate, contact the shift supervisor immediately.   Give a complete description (see step 1 above) of each escapee, the time of the escape, the direction of travel of the escapee(s), whether the escapee(s) are armed, and await instruction. The shift supervisor will notify the appropriate police agency immediately upon receipt of this information. *[1] [3] [5]*

7. The appropriate police agency is responsible for making a complete investigation of the escape and reporting the results to the Commander of Jail Operations. *[10]*

8. Immediately upon apprehension, the suspect will be held in tight security, until the investigating detectives or officers have thoroughly interrogated him or her. When this has been accomplished, psychiatric personnel will be summoned to perform an evaluation of the subject. The shift supervisor will be afforded the opportunity to sit in on any consequent reclassification of the inmate. *[9]*

12. <u>Policy, Procedure, and Task Get Scrambled</u>

Of all the "deadly dozen," the blending of policy, procedure, and task is one of the surest ways to produce a policy-procedure manual that defies reading.

Some policies, procedures, and tasks are so scrambled they belong on a breakfast menu.

Often it's obvious the writer's own mind hasn't clearly distinguished policy, procedure, and task. As a result, the ideas spill onto the page like clothes from a tumble-dryer. Then the readers—if they try at all—must mentally sort out each piece and fit it into its proper place.

The differences that set policy, procedure, and task apart are important differences. They matter because each kind of written direction works best in its own format. Unless you first "think them apart," you won't be able to present each of the three in its own most readable form. What are the differences? That's the subject of the next chapter.

Summary

Twelve common mistakes make policies and procedures hard to read:

WRITING STYLE

1. Sentences Run Too Long

2. Long Words Clog the Flow of Ideas

3. Headings Merely Label—They Say Nothing

4. Lifeless Verbs Add Length and Prompt Yawns

5. Many Doers Disappear

6. Vague Modifiers Create Unanswered Questions

PAGE LAYOUT

7. Pages Cover Too Much

8. Long Paragraphs Turn Readers Away

9. Long Lines Add More Friction

ORGANIZATION

10. Lists Fall from Parallel Form

11. Time Tumbles Out of Order

12. Policy, Procedure, and Task Get Scrambled

Few if any of these pitfalls violate rules from English class. A policy or procedure may suffer from every one of them and yet remain grammatically "correct." But each of the deadly dozen injects its share of poison. Together, they explain why so many manuals fail to direct the actions of employees.

Goal ⟶

To direct the choices actions of employees as they work together or alone to carry out the missions of the organization

Chapter Three:

DEFINITIONS

Policy. Procedure. Task. What's the difference?

A TV channel selector makes it possible to view one program at a time. In a similar way, by separating policy, procedure, and task, you allow the reader to focus on one kind of written direction at a time.

P eople avoid written direction because they can't find answers to practical questions.   Too often, those answers get lost because it appears the writer must have used a blender to "organize" different kinds of material.

So even before you begin to write, you'll need to separate the three basic kinds of written direction. That means sifting out policy from procedure—and both of those from task. This will take some mental work. You'll have to *think* them apart before you can *write* them apart.

Separating the three elements is important because each of the three serves a different purpose.   Each directs the actions of employees, but in its own unique way. And each works best in its own format. When a piece of written direction appears in the layout that suits it best, it's easier to read.   That means it's more likely to be read—and followed.   Let's start with some basic definitions:

Policy: *(rule Book)*
- **Describes a management decision.**
  related to a single work activity

Procedure: *(Play book)*
- **Lists in order the steps a team takes to complete an action loop.** *2 or more people.*

Task Outline: *Detailed action).*
- **Lists in order the steps <u>one person</u> takes to complete a procedure step or a series of related actions.**

Now let's examine each definition, look at an example, and think through its value.

POLICY

A policy *describes a management decision*. Here, think of "management" in its broadest sense. Of course management includes the top-level administrators in your organization. But it also includes any person—or agency—whose decisions dictate what people in your organization must or must not do.

"Management" includes any person or group with authority to issue orders that govern the way work must be done.

For example, the state legislature and local governments pass laws that govern your operations, so they are "management" in this sense. Likewise, court decisions can affect what employees may or must not do. So think of courts, too, as "management" when writing policy.

Once you see policy as "a management decision" you'll see it everywhere in life. The game of football illustrates this well. Many decisions have been made before a game ever starts: the size of the field, the limits on playing time, the number of players on each team, and so on. All of these decisions dictate what players must and must not do during the game. So such decisions are policy.

Football also shows how putting policies in writing saves time. When policy is written down, everyone can refer to it. One properly documented decision can guide an unlimited number of similar actions in the future. Imagine sitting through a football game in which all the rules—height of goal posts, penalties, size of ball, and hundreds of others—had to be re-negotiated before actual play got underway. A sure way to empty the bleachers!

Preserve valuable management decisions on paper: They'll save time.

Well-written policy saves management from re-deciding issues already resolved. So capture those valuable management decisions on paper. They'll save time when employees need to know the approved thing to do in comparable situations.

PROCEDURE

Always show procedure steps in chronological order.

A procedure *lists in order the steps a team takes to complete an action loop*. Let's take that definition apart, piece by piece.

First, procedures *list in order.* To get things done, team members have to know *when* to do their part. A well-written procedure tells them. The best way to do that is simply to list the steps in chronological order, the way they are supposed to happen.

Second, procedures list *steps.* Procedures don't give management decisions (policy) and they don't explain why the steps are necessary.

Procedures always involve two or more people.

Third, procedures list in order the steps *a team takes.* If it doesn't take a team, it isn't a procedure. Write a procedure only when the action sequence involves two or more people. If it involves just one person, it's a task.

Finally, procedures lists in order the steps a team takes to *complete an action loop.* An action loop includes all the steps a team must take as they work together to finish that particular chunk of work.

A "trigger" tells the first team member to "Go!"

Every action loop begins with a "trigger"—a definite starting point, something that tells the first team member to "Go!" And an action loop must have a "target"—a definite final step that tells the last doer to "Stop!"

A "target" tells the last team member to "Stop!"

An action loop can be self-triggering, such as when the first doer simply decides to start the action. Or a trigger can name the event that starts the action sequence. For example, the event of a customer entering a restaurant might set the greeting-seating action loop in motion.

In a relay race, the "trigger" is the starter's pistol. Hearing the shot, the leadoff runner takes the first step, runs a lap, and then "hands off" the action to the next runner, and so on. Finally, the winning runner reaches the "target," the tape.

A procedure works like a relay race--or like a football play.

Meanwhile, back to our football game. The rules written beforehand are policy. The plays the team uses to reach its goal are procedures. Let's follow one of the plays: The quarterback tells the center to snap the ball (that's the trigger). The center snaps the ball to the quarterback. The quarterback fades back and passes the ball to the wide receiver. The wide receiver catches the ball and runs for the touchdown (that's the target).

The central action in that play—the action surrounding that ball—involved three players. Because the effort required more than one person to complete the action loop (reach the goal), that play is easiest to follow when written in the procedure format.

Well written procedures identify *who* will take each action.

Too often, procedures in not-so-effective formats leave out the players. That amounts to a football play written like this: "The ball is snapped to the quarterback. After the fade back is completed, the ball is passed to the wide receiver. Then the run is made and the touchdown is scored." The doers in such vaguely written procedures are "missing in action." And so the real doers may turn out to be no-shows when it's time to take action.

People value clear, concise, and easy-to-read directions. With such procedures everyone knows what to do, who will do each part, and in what sequence. That kind of awareness helps teams reach their goals.

TASK OUTLINE

A task outline *lists in order the steps one person takes to complete a procedure step or a series of related actions*. The key to that definition is *one person*. If the work remains in the hands of just one person for more than five or six steps, it's a task, not a procedure.

A task outline is a solo, a "procedure for one."

One more trip to the football field. Suppose the quarterback needs instruction on how to pass the football. A task outline would provide a sequential list of how-to-pass details: How to accept the snap, how to grip the football properly, how to stand, how to find a receiver, and how to launch the pass. The rest of the team will appreciate it if the writer leaves out of the procedure these fine points about passing—information no one but the quarterback will use.

A task is often triggered by a procedure step. The center snaps the ball, triggering the passing task. Yes, the snap is also a step in the procedure. But as a task trigger, the snap simply sets up the context in which the quarterback carries out those how-to-pass directions. The center's snap serves as the "Go" signal for the quarterback's task.

In some cases, though, a task outline simply lists a series of related actions—actions not directly connected with a procedure. For example, a scorekeeper at a football game works alone and not as part of the 11-member team who carry out the plays. But the scorekeeper may need instructions on the series of related actions required to complete a form. That series would make up a task outline.

Let's restate all this as simply as we can:

Policy: What should be done.

Procedure: Who does what—and when.

Task Outline: How to do it.

Now, with those in mind, read the example in the right-hand column of the next few pages. Identify the policy, procedure, and task information that you find. Then compare your conclusions with the comments in the left-hand column.

Task outlines come in two types:

(1) A detailed breakdown of one procedure step, and

(2) A series of steps unrelated to any procedure.

Transporting Persons in Custody

General

The transportation of probation and parole violators is a normal probation and parole officer function. As a general rule, the extradition and return of a parole violator from another state is handled by the division, while the return of a probation violator is a responsibility of the county of conviction. Probationers are more frequently transported for short distances within the state. County authorities should be encouraged to accept this responsibility. If they do not, the Probation and Parole Division may transport probationers.

Most of this consists of what <u>management</u> has <u>decided</u> about who is responsible for various kinds of transports. So this is <u>policy</u>.

The transporting of a violator from another state is coordinated by the deputy compact administrator in headquarters. While most out-of-state prisoner

Some <u>procedure</u> begins to appear here.

The titles of several people begin to appear—suggesting a <u>team</u>. And if it takes a team, it takes a <u>procedure</u>.

transports are handled by the <u>transportation officer</u> located in the headquarters office, <u>probation and parole officers</u> occasionally make these trips when the transportation officer is unable to do so. The <u>probation and parole officer</u> to be assigned to transport is selected by a <u>supervisor</u>, with the officer who is supervising the case given the first consideration. Workload factors and officer preferences are considered. For potentially hazardous transports, a <u>staff member</u> with sufficient experience and physical strength is selected. Written instructions (see example 20.587) and other necessary documents are provided to the <u>officer</u> by the <u>deputy compact administrator</u>.

This is pure <u>task</u>: it tells <u>one person</u>—the transporting officer— how to carry out the transport task.

Prisoners who are being returned are frequently anxious and concerned about their situation. It is natural that the conversation between the prisoner and the <u>officer</u> turns to this subject. The <u>officer</u> should avoid offering judgments, opinions, or predictions of what may happen to the prisoner. Admonishing, arguing, or talking to the prisoner in a way that might evoke antagonism is to be avoided. It is important that conversation be as pleasant and relaxed as possible to keep from increasing the prisoner's anxiety.

Here's a little explanation, a little philosophizing, and a little <u>task</u>.

While there are general guidelines governing transporting prisoners, there are too many variables for them to cover all situations. Good organization and appropriate planning of the transport will reduce the frequency and lessen the difficulty of dealing with unanticipated developments. A fundamental precept is to obtain assistance as soon as a need to do so is apparent. The deputy compact administrator in headquarters may be called at any time for advice. A transporting <u>officer</u> should not be hesitant in placing a prisoner in a detention facility and/or restraints when time is needed to resolve a problem, or when the security of the prisoner or other persons is the least bit questionable.

Some more <u>policy</u> and some more <u>task</u>.

Use of restraints is <u>mandatory</u> during all phases of the transport except in detention cells, and in court rooms and aircraft where restraints are not permitted. In the event the use of restraints aboard an aircraft is deemed necessary, <u>this is to be cleared</u> with the captain. The usual restraints used for transporting are handcuffs and "belly chains" or "waistraints."

Legal Authority to Transport

This is mostly background and explanation. The last sentence hints at a <u>procedure</u> because it says "the officer" will be instructed. That suggests a <u>team</u>, the officer and the person doing the instructing. But the sentence doesn't tell us who that person is.

It is essential that officers have formal material to assure the transfer of custody of prisoners or transporting purposes and for subsequent use in booking prisoners into other facilities. The officer must have official agency identification and a warrant or an order authorizing the detention which is acceptable to a receiving facility. For cases being returned from other states, additional material includes a formal warrant and extradition papers or a waiver of extradition. On occasion a transport will be arranged without the signed waiver in hand. This is sometimes done in the interest of time when a teletype message is received from the retaining agency stating that the individual has signed a waiver of extradition. In this event the <u>officer</u> will <u>be instructed</u> to pick up copies of the signed waiver in the other state.

There is nothing but background here--an explanation of what the law means.

There are three general types of legal means by which a person is transported between states: 1) cases where extradition is not an issue; 2) cases formally extradited; and 3) cases where extradition has been legally waived. Every person scheduled for return to this state in custody has a right through legal means to resist being returned. If that right is not waived, extradition procedures are initiated. If extradition is allowed, the person is returned over his or her objection.

More background and more and more. Finally, the last sentence implies the work of a <u>team</u>, so we'll call it part of a <u>procedure</u>.

There are two ways that extradition may be waived. Either the person must have signed a waiver of extradition prior to leaving the state or voluntarily sign new waivers at the time return is requested. The waivers signed prior to the person leaving the state are processed through the procedures of the Interstate Compact for the Supervision of Probationers and parolees. Extradition papers, the Rendition Warrant, or the waivers of extradition usually have been processed by the Interstate Compact authorities prior to a transporting officer becoming involved, with appropriate copies provided to the officer along with other documents. While a prisoner may have waived extradition or may be extradited, a court appearance may be a routine formality or may be necessary to resolve some point. Occasionally, courts are not familiar with their own state's Interstate Compact laws. If it appears that a problem is developing in the other

state, this should <u>be reported</u> to the appropriate <u>deputy compact administrator</u> in the headquarters office immediately by telephone.

Summary

To avoid scrambling policy, procedure, and task together, you need to understand clearly the differences that separate the three kinds of direction.

Policy:

> **Describes a management decision. (What should be done.)**

Procedure:

> **Lists in order the steps a team takes to complete an action loop. (Who does what—and when.)**

Task Outline:

> **Lists in order the steps one person takes to complete a procedure step or a series of related actions. (How to do it.)**

- An *action loop* includes all the steps a team takes to reach a goal.

- A *trigger* initiates each action loop.

- A *target* ends each action loop.

Chapter Four:

POLICIES

How to coax a policy out of your head and onto paper.

As we saw in Chapter Three, the first step in writing policy is thinking—mentally separating the raw material of policy from that of procedures and tasks. This thinking step must occur before the second step, writing the policy for others to read. This chapter follows that two-step process.

The first section explains how to use the *Policy Planner* to organize your thoughts as you draft policies. (See the master copy in your Writer's Kit at the end of this book.) The *Planner* helps you identify policy because it's designed to filter out procedure and task material. You may copy the blank master copy of the *Planner* whenever you need a fresh supply.

This two-part chapter offers help first with planning policies, then with writing them.

Part Two introduces another tool, the *Policy Layout and Writing Guide*, a checklist to use when you write policies. Again, your Writer's Kit includes a master copy. The *Guide* will help you avoid the writing mistakes that make the average policy so hard to read. It will also remind you how to write policies in the easy-to-read "headline" format you will learn in this chapter.

Part One: Planning a Policy

You'll find a master copy of the *Policy Planner* in the back of this book.

Livable houses don't happen without carefully drawn blueprints. Workable policies don't happen without thoughtfully created plans. A good plan emerges from many tentative jottings, refinements, fresh starts, and recombinations. In other words, planning is messy and time-consuming. But by planning how to plan, you can make the process at least somewhat more efficient. The *Policy Planner* is designed to keep you on track as you plan your policy. Before you begin, make several blank copies of the *Planner* to use as work sheets.

To write a policy, start by making notes to yourself on a blank *Planner*. It offers four prompts to help you organize key policy elements:

1. *Write a title in six words or less that covers the activity and distinguishes it from other activities.*

2. *Describe the boundaries of this policy.*

3. *List your main points (with any exceptions). Management has decided that . . . (except when) . . .*

4. *Write the name of the person who will sign (or otherwise approve) the policy.*

The next few pages will explain how to use each of those prompts. You may want to refer to the blank *Policy Planner* in your Writer's Kit to see where the responses fit. You'll also find a filled-in example of the *Planner* on page 36.

A completed Policy Planner is included on page 36 as an example.

1. Write a title in six words or less that covers the activity and distinguishes it from other activities.

This six-word limit leaves no room for filler words. Every word must pack punch. After you've created a short, no-nonsense title, the reader will be able to grasp it in a flash.

To keep yourself from writing a title that covers too much, you'll need to distinguish between *service areas* and *activities*.

Write your policy titles to describe specific work *activities*, not the overall *services* you provide.

• *Service Areas*. Think of some broad categories in which your organization provides useful help. If you own a restaurant, "Meals" and "Atmosphere" would be services to your diners. "Maintenance" would be a service to your building. Those are *service areas*—ways in which your work supplies something of value to others.

• *Activities*. Now think of the *activities* required to provide those services. To provide a "Meals" service requires many activities: Planning Menus, Ordering Ingredients, Preparing Food, Washing Dishes, and so on. To provide the "Atmosphere" service requires such activities as Isolating Smokers, Controlling Room Temperature, and Removing Unruly Guests.

In each of the examples above, notice this: the word that describes the activity ends in -*ing*. Plan*ning*, order*ing*, prepar*ing*, and so on. It will clarify your own thinking--and communicate that clarity to the reader--if the first word in your policy title is a verb that ends in -*ing*.

Write your policy title at the *activity* level. The *service area* will usually include far more activities than one policy can effectively communicate. When custodians report in for work, they are not looking for directions on how to do "maintenance" (the overall service provided). Instead, they want directions for carrying out specific *activities*—washing windows, emptying wastebaskets, or replacing light bulbs. So by writing your title at that activity level, you are describing exactly what the reader is looking for. The title is the "handlebar" by which the reader can get a grip on the management decisions.

A helpful title will give away both what the policy includes and what it excludes.

Take the time to create a title that exactly defines the activity your policy *includes*. But make sure the title also marks the policy's edges or boundaries—what it *excludes*. No one wants to read completely through a policy only to find that the needed information must be somewhere else.

For example, if our policy on prisoner transport covered only in-state transport, the title should reflect that restriction. If it covers both in-state and out-of-state, then a more general title would work—perhaps "Transporting Probation and Parole Violators." That still distinguishes it from another policy on transferring inmates from one prison to another (which might be called "Relocating Inmates").

2. Describe the boundaries of this policy.

Here, you will describe the borders of the policy in more detail than was possible in the title. As you complete this section, ask yourself the same questions about applying the policy that your readers will probably ask themselves. Does it apply to both in-state and out-of-state transport? Does it apply equally to transporting probation and parole violators?

As you supply the answers to such questions, you will be creating a "scope statement" that tells the reader how far the policy reaches. Later, when you write it into the format, this scope statement will appear just below the title. By using both the title and this statement, the reader should be able to answer these three questions:

- Who is (and is not) covered by this policy?
- Where does (and doesn't) this policy apply?
- When does (and doesn't) this policy apply?

3. List your main points *(with any exceptions)*. Management has decided that . . . *(except when: . . .)*

The words "Management has decided that . . ." work as a "filter" to help you sift out policy decisions from other material. Just complete the sentence, and you will probably have discovered a piece of policy

The sequence of management decisions doesn't matter on the *Policy Planner*. You can rearrange the order as you write the first draft.

Don't worry about the order at this stage. The *Policy Planner* provides space for six decisions. You may not need them all. If you need more than six, continue on a separate sheet of paper. No matter how many it takes, write out statements that summarize the main management decisions in this activity.

A look at the example on page 36 shows that some of the information from the original piece on prisoner transportation didn't show up on the *Planner*. That's because much of the material under "Legal Authority to Transport" didn't qualify as a management decision.

For example, the original version describes three legal ways to transport a violator between states. This won't vary from state to state and isn't something management in this state decided anyway. The information might be useful in a training session on the extradition process. But it bogs down a working manual and makes it hard for readers to find the decision-making directions they need.

Perhaps a decision applies in most—but not all—cases. In the "except when" space, describe the special cases so the reader knows when *not* to follow a standard course of action.

Some decisions are beyond management's control. For example, if the county authorities won't cooperate by transporting a violator within the state, then a state official may have to do the job instead. And if an airline refuses to allow a prisoner to fly while handcuffed, then the regular policy on restraints will have to be suspended for that part of the trip.

If the same exceptions appear repeatedly, consider writing a separate policy to cover those situations. For example, if you find yourself writing "except when out of state" for the umpteenth time, write a separate policy that gives directions for out-of-state transports. This will sweep out the clutter of exceptions.

4. Write the name or title of the person who will sign (or otherwise approve) the policy.

Some firms with online document systems don't use signatures to authenticate policies and procedures.

Only one name or title has practical value to the reader—that of the person who can authorize the policy as the approved set of rules governing this activity. Identify that person, and include his or her name or title on the *Planner*.

So much for the theory and advice on policy planning. Now look at a completed sample *Planner*. Your first reaction might very well be: "You mean that's all there is to it? It looks so short in comparison with the original."

Two things explain this brevity: First, it leaves out all procedure and task material. That strips away much of the wordiness that helped turn the original into verbal quicksand. Second, the items listed on the policy planner are just rough thinking notes. The final version—written from these notes—will restore some of the length. But writing the final version is the subject of the second part of this chapter.

POLICY PLANNER

1. **Write a title in six words or less that describes the activity and distinguishes it from other activities.**

   Transporting Probation and Parole Violators

2. **Describe the boundaries of this policy.**

   Applies to all extraditions, parole, and probation violations.

   Applies to both in-state and out-of-state transports.

3. **List your main points** *(with any exceptions).* **Management has decided**

   that State PPOs normally handle extraditions, out-of-state returns.

   (except when: _____)

   that County authorities should handle in-state transports

   (except when: County authorities refuse—then PPOs handle in-state transports)

   that the Deputy Compact Administrator coordinates all transports

   (except when: _____)

   that restraints will be used during all transports

   (except when: airline rules prohibit passengers from traveling in restraints)

   that _____

   (except when: _____)

   that _____

   (except when: _____)

4. **Write the name or title of the person who will sign (or otherwise approve) this policy.** Director Jones

Summary of Part One: Planning a Policy

- Policies tell everyone in the organization what management decisions govern a specific activity.

- The blank *Policy Planner* in the Writer's Kit (p. 110) will help organize your thinking by providing key information in four areas.

- Write a short title—six words or less. It should describe the work activity the reader will do. The first word of the title should end in *-ing*.

- Describe the policy boundaries (p. 33). What people, places, times, and so on does it cover and not cover?

- List management decisions and any exceptions. The phrase "Management has decided that . . . " will help you sort out policy from procedure and task.

- Write the name or title of the person who will authorize the policy.

Part Two: Writing a Policy

Once you've captured the main management decisions on a *Policy Planner*, you're ready for the next step: putting them on paper in a form everyone can understand easily. And accurately.

Use the *Guide* as a working checklist. Make as many copies as you need and keep one in view as you write. Use it after you write to review your work.

Another tool in your Writer's Kit will help you do that: the *Policy Layout and Writing Guide*. By following its 10 guidelines and checking your policy draft against its seven "checksteps," you'll avoid the typical mistakes found in written policies. As a preview, here are the 10 guidelines:

1. *Use a standard header to provide clear and useful information at the top of each page.*

2. *Start each policy on a new page.*

3. *Write and rewrite a title until it describes the policy and separates it from similar policies.*

4. *Sum up management decisions in sentence headlines.*

5. *Make page layout work for your readers, not against them.*

6. *Limit paragraph length to 10 typed lines.*

7. *Limit average sentence length to 17 words or less.*

8. *Limit "long" words to 10 percent or less of your total word count.*

9. *Make at least 10 percent of your words work as active verbs.*

10. *Signal any revision with an asterisk keyed to a brief explanation at the bottom of the page.*

Each guideline needs some explanation. The following sections describe all ten in more detail and show how to use them with actual examples.

1. Use a standard header to provide clear and useful information at the top of each page.

A "header" is a standard arrangement of key information that goes at the top—or "head"—of a policy. Good headers help your policies work like a well-organized toolbox—with all the essentials in predictable places.

Develop a compact design that delivers the important information clearly and then use it on all your policies. Soon your readers will be able to find key information quickly by scanning.

Avoid these four common mistakes in policy headers:

A. Inconsistency. Inconsistent headers make your readers feel like you rearranged their office furniture without asking them first. The confusion will cause them to spend more time on the header than on the policy itself.

B. Incompleteness. Some headers give too little information—like the one that contains no clue as to what earlier policy it cancels or the one that doesn't say when the policy took effect.

For longer policies, headers on page two and any pages that follow can be simpler than the first. They need only tie the later pages to the first.

C. *Overkill.* Sometimes headers burst with useless information. For example, it does the reader no good to see the names of the dozen people who reviewed a policy before it was issued. Those names may help the writer defend the process used to issue the policy if someone challenges it—so the names belong in the document history file. But the reader needs only an assurance of official approval

For headers, simpler is almost always the better choice.

D. *Clutter.* Still others go overboard with graphic designs, becoming visual junkyards, so crowded with lines and dots and fancy fonts that the reader has trouble spotting the useful nuggets.

Find a compact, graphically appealing way to arrange the following elements at the top of your policies (with, perhaps, your organizational logo as well):

• *POLICY*—Make this word stand out from the other header elements with a larger typeface or a color. Then even readers new to your system will know what they've found.

• *Effective Date*—This tells when to begin using this version of the policy. Which means readers should have it well before this date.

• *Page X of Y*—Tells the reader at once how many pages make up the complete policy. Since pages do get lost, this can be critical.

If your "see also" lists tend to be long and disrupt your headers, move them to the end of the policy.

• *Cancels*—Shows the number and date of any policies this one supersedes (including previous versions of this policy).

• *See Also*—To understand a policy completely, a reader might need to refer to other policies, procedures, or task outlines. If so, list them here.

Other possible elements:

• *Approved by*—If you want your policies signed, provide a place for the signature on the first page of each policy. A policy is normally approved by the highest-ranking person in the division or department that will use it.

• *Manual/Directory*—You may need more than one manual or online directory for policies and procedures. If so, the reader must be able to see which manual or directory each policy is from. Even with an on-line document system, make sure the header supplies the directory\subdirectory so readers can find the document again on the system.

2. Start each policy on a new page.

This guideline serves both you and your readers. First, readers will find it easier to locate policies in a manual if your format always puts the header at the top of a new page. Too many manuals cram as much as possible on a page, sometimes covering two or even three policy areas on a single page. Starting each new policy on a fresh sheet may cost you a few extra pages. But what you gain in reading ease will more than offset the extra paper.

Saving paper at the expense of readability is no saving. Better to leave half pages blank than to have whole pages unread.

Second, starting each new policy on a new page simplifies your revision process. Each policy becomes self-contained and thus unaffected if you add or delete pages from neighboring policies.

If you use a computerized document system, separate each individual policy into its own file. Even though you're using a powerful word processor or document management program, it's a needless chore to sift through several policies in the same file.

3. Write and rewrite the title until it describes the policy and separates it from others that may be similar.

You created a working title on the policy planner. Now give it some critical thought. Can you improve on it? Many policy titles try to cover too much ground. Readers expect a title to help them find the directions they need right away. The title, one of many in a table of contents, must give away as much as possible about the content of the whole policy. To make a title say more, narrow its focus.

Difficulty focusing the title may be a clue that the policy is too broad. Try breaking the title up to describe more than one activity.

Here's a title that tries to circle the earth:

Communication, Mail, and Visiting

That title suggests a policy that covers three major areas related only by an abstract idea (contact with persons outside a prison). So it doesn't help readers learn whether this policy will answer their specific questions.

Even if you break these into three policies, the subjects are still too general. The word "visiting," for example, describes a service area, not an activity done by employees of the prison. The prison provides "visiting" as a service to prisoners, their families, and friends. But to make the visiting service available, employees must be engaged in certain activities, such as "Approving Additions to Visitor Lists," or "Scheduling Visits by Family Members."

4. Sum up management decisions in sentence headlines.

The headline format makes even complex policies easy to read quickly.

Headlines make it easy for readers to grasp your main management decisions quickly and correctly. Look at the format example on page 43. The headlines stand out because they jut into the white space to the left and because the blank lines above and below separate them from the text. Such high-visibility headlines make your management decisions hard to miss.

When you write a headline, make sure you state the management decision—don't just label it. To state it, express it in a sentence. If your headline has no subject or verb, chances are you've written only a label. The original examples below are marked *label*. The revised examples are marked *headline*. Notice the difference a sentence can make.

(label) **Cost of Clothing Issue**

(headline) **Prison Provides up to $100 of Clothing**

See how verbs (*provides, approves, vary*) make the difference between merely labeling an idea and really expressing it?

(label) **Annual Leave Approval**

(headline) **Supervisor Approves Annual Leave**

(label) **Children**

(headline) **Minors' Visiting Rules Vary by Age**

Study those examples as if you were the reader, and you'll see why the revisions work better. They allow the reader to get the main ideas faster and more accurately. Why? Because sentence headlines preview the text, sum it up, and prepare the reader to understand detail in context.

The sentence headline technique works powerfully. As you practice using it, keep two points in mind:

Always include a verb. No End Marks. Bold Face

- *Keep your headlines short, ideally under ten words.* This helps harried readers grasp your points in an instant.

- *Use headlines generously.* If the headline states all you need to say, let it stand alone without any text below. Don't add text just to make the page look weighty or because the headline looks "lonely" by itself.

5. Make page layout work for your readers, not against them.

Your page layout can send a mixed message. The fact that you've taken the trouble to write a policy sends one message: "Read this." But if you're not careful, your page layout—the way you arrange titles, headlines, and text— may send another: "Don't bother."

Don't overdo capitalized words. They are harder to read than words in both UPPER and lower case.

Make each page invite the reader's eye. One look at the page, and the reader should relish the prospect of reading it, not recoil from it. You can raise the general attractiveness and readability of your policies by observing a few simple guidelines on format. The next page shows how title, text, and headlines can be arranged effectively, with notes on how to use upper and lower case.

POL-### — <u>TITLE ALL IN BOLD CAPITALS AND UNDERLINED</u>

[handwritten: Block Indent →] This introductory text (the "scope" statement based on item #2 from your Policy Planner) is block-indented from the left in normal print. Right margins are ragged to avoid spreading and compressing letters with full justification. Maximum text width: five inches.

1. **<u>First Headline in Bold Initial Capitals and Underlined</u>**

   This text, also indented, lets the headline stand out. Use "initial capitals." That means capitalizing nouns, pronouns, and verbs as well as other words over four letters. Capitalize articles (the, an, a) and prepositions (to, from, with, etc.) only when they are the first words.

2. **<u>Second Headline in Bold Initial Capitals and Underlined</u>**

   All headlines at the same level should use the same layout features (typeface, capitalization, indenting). Readers depend on these cues to help them understand the relationship between the policy points.

This layout raises the visibility of each element of the policy. Titles and subheadings stand out because they're in **bold, <u>underlined,</u>** and because they reach into the white space in the left margin. And the text—in short, scannable lines—promises an easy read.

6. Limit paragraph length to 10 typed lines.

[handwritten: On line keep to 5 lines.]

Readers resist bloated paragraphs. Faced with one, they often "check out" after the first line or so. They usually don't "check in" again until their eyes find a fresh paragraph break.

[handwritten: Vary size of paragraph.]

Follow this guideline and you won't have to worry about losing readers because of overstuffed paragraphs. No, there's nothing magic about ten lines. An 11- or 12-line paragraph probably won't bother most readers. But it will help you, the writer, to have a measurable standard in mind. Keeping your paragraphs at or under 10 lines will prevent many more problems than it creates.

7. Limit average sentence length to 17 words or less.

Getting through some sentences is like running a marathon—you have to be in top shape to reach the end! For decades readability researchers have agreed that overly long sentences confuse readers. In their book, *Know Your Reader*, George R. Klare and Byron Buck say "Almost every study points to the importance of sentence length in affecting how well writing can be understood."

This guideline reflects what research shows about sentence length and reading comprehension. Follow it and you will eliminate a major cause of readers' problems. But how do you shrink a sentence already out of control? First, examine each "marathon" sentence until you see what's stretching it. Then, once you've found the cause, the cure should suggest itself.

In one study, every reader could follow sentences averaging eight words. Ninety-seven percent understood those that averaged 17 words. Above that, reader comprehension dropped sharply.

Look for three all-too-common causes when a sentence "just keeps going, and going, and going . . . ."

A. Sentences that make pointless points.

This example comes from a policy governing a prison law library:

If an inmate is deemed indigent and does not have available funds, then the library staff will be authorized to photocopy items requested without charging a fee. (28 words)

By definition, an "indigent" does not have available funds. Use either the term or its definition—it is pointless to use both. And the word "requested" isn't needed—the staff makes copies only on request. Similarly, "charging" already suggests the "fee."

Why not reduce the whole sentence to less than half the length while still putting the point across. Like this:

If an inmate cannot pay, the library staff may provide photocopies without charge. (13 words)

Here's a second reason sentences run on and on:

B. Subjects and verbs that come too late.

Sometimes, writers make the reader wait too long before reaching the subject and verb—the words that bring all others into focus. Example:

Only with the approval of a security official (of the rank of correctional supervisor or above), who shall evaluate the grounds asserted to justify the search will visitors be requested to submit to such further searches. (36 words)

If the readers stick with it they'll eventually find that the subject is *visitors* and the verb is *will ... be.* But few readers will plow through the first 26 words, especially since those words give little clue about where the sentence is heading. And even fewer will remember what those 26 words said by the time they reach the subject and verb.

In English, verbs "push" better than they "pull." So put the verb right after the subject most of the time.

The cure? Move the acting subject up and put it at or near the beginning of the sentence. Then follow it closely with the active verb. If necessary, use more than one sentence, like this:

A staff member may ask visitors to submit to further search only if a security official (correction supervisor or above) approves. The security official will evaluate whether there are valid reasons for further search. (34 words, with a 17 words-per-sentence average.)

Finally, a third cause of meandering sentences:

C. Too many ideas compete for attention.

In the late 1800s, L. A. Sherman, an English Professor in the University of Nebraska, made the first real study of sentence lengths. He concluded that writers with the clearest style used sentences that carried "One mind-full at a time." Now, a century later, many writers have apparently never heard Sherman's advice. So all too often readers still stumble upon sentences like this:

When an individual is approved for time payments or short-term court time payments and subsequently fails to make their payment, a criminal complaint is issued charging them with failure to pay-appear and

15 days subsequent to the criminal complaint a warrant will be issued charging them with failure to pay-appear. (53 words)

Why not give readers the same ideas one "mind-full at a time"?

If a person fails to make a payment on time, the court will issue a criminal complaint. This complaint will charge the person with failure to pay or appear. Fifteen days after issuing the complaint, the court will issue a warrant on the same charge. (45 words, 15 word-per-sentence average)

8. Limit "long" words to 10 percent or less of your total word count.

Readers are not insulted by "easy" writing. Like running, reading is hard work. You don't often choose to run at your top speed—or to read material that strains you to the limit.

In recent decades, readability researchers have devised ways to estimate reading ease. Today, the major word processing programs include built-in tools for testing reading difficulty. Two of the best-known tests (the *Flesch Readability Formula* and the *Gunning Fog Index*) use word length as a key way to measure reading difficulty. The higher the percentage of long words, the more difficult the reader's job.

This guideline—no more than 10 percent "long" words—provides an objective standard for your writing. The 10-percent-long-word-limit works hand in hand with the 17-word-average-sentence-length-limit of guideline #7. If you write a policy with only 10 percent long words and with sentences that average 17 words, someone with an 11th grade reading skill should be able to read it easily. (That's according to the *Gunning Fog Index*. And that's assuming what you write makes sense.)

Most adults don't like to read material written at grade levels of difficulty over 11—and many simply can't read it. Follow the limits of guidelines #7 and #8, and you'll greatly increase the chance your readers will read and understand.

To simplify the math, use 100 word samples to check your writing. Just count out 100 words, and then tally the number of words in the sample that have three or more syllables. If you find more than 10, substitute shorter words. But not all words of three or more syllables count

Website: www.readabilityformulas.com — use free Calculator down too below.

as "long." The exceptions are: *Proper nouns; combinations of short words; and three-syllable words ending in "-es" or "-ed."*

• *Proper nouns.* Capitalized words that name a specific person, place, or thing don't count as long words, no matter how many syllables. Examples: *Department of Licensing; Columbia River; Special Rehabilitation Facility; Mississippi.*

• *Combinations of short words.* A word isn't "long" if it just combines some small words. Examples: *paperwork; understand; database.*

• *Three-syllable words ending in "-es" or "-ed."* Because of this exception, you would not count these as "long": *reduces; appointed; detailed.* (But do count four-syllable and longer words that end in -es or -ed—words like *violated; implemented; recognizes.*)

9. Make at least 10 percent of your words work as active verbs.

Passive verbs inflate writing and make it flabby.

Active verbs produce crisper, clearer policies. But too many of us habitually rely on passive verbs instead of active ones. This section will show you how to measure the "verbal activity level" in your writing. First, we'll cover the verbs you *won't* count. Second, the verbs you *will.*

A. Inactive Verbs: Don't Count Them

1. Don't count any form of the verb "to be" (*am, are, is, was, were, be, been*) unless it is followed by a word ending in "-ing":

Rules and regulations <u>are</u> essential to the efficient operation of any agency.

This letter <u>is</u> in response to your letter of December 12.

(But in **"I <u>am responding</u> to your letter,"** the *am* followed by *responding* count as one active verb.)

2. Don't count the verb-like word that follows a "to be" verb.

1. What's really happening here?
2. Who or what what makes it happen?

Extradition may **be waived** in two ways.

The prisoners **were required** to submit to searching.

B. Active Verbs: Count Them

1. Count a "to be" verb as active if it teams up with a word ending in "-ing."

This kind of a verb counts as active because it requires an acting doer as its subject. The word ending in "-ing" often suggests an extended period of action:

The Administrative Segregation Committee is delaying its decision.

The Sheriff's Office and the City Police were jointly investigating the murder.

2. Count each infinitive (except for "to be").

An infinitive is a verb preceded by the word "to." Examples: *to think; to consider; to penalize; to plan; to run; to decide.*

I am asking you to approve this parole plan.

You will need to review the new jail blue-prints and identify required changes.

Notice that in the last example the second "to" (as in *to identify*) doesn't show, but is implied.

3. Count each verb that appears after its "doer" and tells what the "doer" does, did, or will do.

In some sentences the "doer" will be a person. In others, the "doer" may be an inanimate thing that doesn't actually do the action, but we often speak as if it does.

The record lacks enough evidence for a solid case.

The schedule will meet the five-day deadline.

Please evaluate this parole plan.

In the third example, the doer, "you," is implied at the beginning.

Now let's apply those criteria to a paragraph taken from a court's written policy. After each verb you'll see a number in brackets. That number corresponds to one of the numbered comments following the paragraph. How well can you identify the active verbs?

Rules and regulations are [1] essential to the efficient operation of any agency. They are [2] necessary for the orderly operation of the Court and for the benefit and safety of all court employees. The court recognizes [3] its responsibility to develop [4] and administer [5] regulations and to be [6] fair and uniform in its handling of personnel disciplinary matters. It is [7] the policy of management to be [8] tolerant and to seek [9] corrective rather than punitive solutions. The primary intention of the court's disciplinary policy is [10] to encourage [11] employees to fulfill [12] responsibilities to court operations in compliance with appropriate regulations, guidelines, and contracts. Inappropriate breaches of court regulations will be dealt [13] with firmly under the uniform procedures which apply [14] to all departments and to all individuals.

> [1] passive verb (a form of "to be")
> [2] passive verb (a form of "to be")
> [3] active verb (the court does the recognizing)
> [4] active verb (infinitive)
> [5] active verb (infinitive, "to" implied)
> [6] passive verb (to be)
> [7] passive verb (one form of "to be")
> [8] passive verb (to be)
> [9] active verb (infinitive)
> [10] passive verb (one of the "to be" verbs)
> [11] active verb (infinitive)
> [12] active verb (infinitive)
> [13] passive verb (verb-like word with "to be")
> [14] active verb (procedures do the applying)

Write actively and you'll write briefly. And more clearly.

That sample of 121 words has just seven active verbs. Dividing seven by 121 gives you about 5.8 percent—far short of the 10 percent this guideline calls for.

Now read the same policy statement written with a higher percentage of active verbs. Compare its reading ease with that of the original.

This court <u>must have</u> rules <u>to conduct</u> its work in an orderly, efficient manner and <u>to protect</u> each member of its staff. In handling staff discipline, we <u>will apply</u> the rules fairly, equally, and with tolerance. We <u>will use</u> the rules <u>to correct</u> rather than <u>to punish</u>. By stating them, we <u>intend</u> <u>to help</u> employees <u>comply</u> with all rules, guidelines and contracts that <u>govern</u> their conduct. We <u>will deal</u> firmly, using our uniform procedures, with anyone who <u>breaks</u> court rules.

This version of the policy has 13 active verbs, 16 percent of the total words used. Notice what happened to the length: 80 words instead of 121. Just activating the verbs helped reduce the verbiage by one-third.

10. **Signal any revision with an asterisk keyed to a brief explanation at the bottom of the page.**

The rewritten policy on transporting prisoners (page 53) illustrates this method of showing changes from an earlier version. Place the asterisk slightly above and to the right of any paragraph that may have changed. If the whole page includes revisions, put the asterisk at the end of the title.

Locate the answering asterisk below the text at the bottom of the page. Follow it with a short description of the kind of change that took place between versions. For example:

* paragraph revised
* paragraph deleted
* new paragraph
* general revision

For the busy reader, these notations provide a way to compare the new with the old without wasting time.

The Checksteps

After drafting your policy with these 10 guidelines, review your work in light of the "checkstep" questions on the right of the *Policy Layout and Writing Guide*. The paragraphs below explain the reason for each checkstep.

1. Is this policy permanent?

Don't overwork your manual—your system for issuing long-term direction—with short-term policies. For example, if you're writing a policy on the structure and functioning of an *ad hoc* committee that will disappear in three months, leave it out of the manual. Issue short-lived directions like that in memo form.

Issuing policies in haste to correct a momentary problem weakens all the rest.

2. Will it relieve management of making similar decisions case-by-case?

Example: Do managers often spend time deciding whether to send employees to conferences? With a clear policy to guide them, supervisors could easily make those decisions without having to involve managers each time. If a policy won't lighten management's decision-making load, ask yourself again whether you should issue it.

3. Is it a valid guide in more than 90 percent of all similar situations?

When you commit a policy to writing, it ought to serve in nearly all cases when employees must choose what to do in that activity. If too many variables make it impossible to write a concise policy that applies consistently, perhaps the best policy will be "Ask your supervisor."

4. Will applying the policy result in fair treatment for everyone involved?

Apply this "fair treatment" question to every person and group affected by the policy: staff, inmates, arrestees, vendors, the public, etc. If it's unfair, it's bad policy.

5. Does it fully convey what management has decided on the issue?

Did you thoroughly cover all decisions that apply to this activity? Or does some area of "unwritten policy" still need to be captured and put on paper? Your readers will soon stop respecting your policies if they find incomplete directions.

6. Are any references missing?

Read each part of the policy with various readers in mind. Would it help any reader to include a reference to another policy, a procedure, or a task? Should the reference be given "on the spot" in parentheses? Or should it appear after the "See Also..." line in the header?

7. Did you cover all exceptions?

Exceptions are easy to miss. So ponder this question before you issue the final draft. Think through the variety of situations readers will face as they try to follow each management decision. For example, thinking through the possible modes of travel in transporting a prisoner would make it obvious that the decision on restraints may not work on a commercial aircraft.

After the following summary, this chapter ends with the rewritten policy on transporting prisoners, which we first saw in Chapter One.

Summary of Part Two: Writing a Policy

- Apply what reading researchers have found to make your policies as "reader-friendly" as possible.

- Use a standard header to give readers all they need—but no more—in a format they can count on.

- Start a new page for each new policy.

- Make each title describe exactly the activity it covers.

- Use sentence headlines generously.

- Keep text lines to no more than five inches wide.

- Break up any paragraph that runs more than 10 lines.

- Use no more than 10 percent "long" words.

- Put at least 10 percent of your words to work as active verbs.

<table>
<tr><td>Effective Date:</td><td rowspan="2">POLICY</td><td>Page: of</td></tr>
</table>

Effective Date: **Page:** of

POLICY

Cancels:

See Also: *Last Revised:*   *or Revise by:*   **Approved by:** _____

POL-321 TRANSPORTING PROBATION AND PAROLE VIOLATORS

This policy applies whenever any officer is assigned to transport a person in custody, either in state or across state lines.

1. Deputy Compact Administrator Coordinates All Transports

The deputy compact administrator (DCA) in headquarters will
- Schedule all transports.
- Obtain any legal documents required to authorize the transport.
- Provide written instructions for the transporting officer to use.

2. State Transportation Officers Usually Conduct Out-of-State Transports [*]

When interstate travel is required, the DCA will usually assign a state transportation officer to accompany the prisoner. However, the DCA may assign a Probation and Parole Officer (PPO) to an interstate transport.

3. County Authorities Should Conduct In-State Transports

The DCA will urge county officials to transport probation violators between counties within this state. If a county official refuses to transport a prisoner within the state, the DCA may assign a state PPO to the task.

4. Restraints Are Required Throughout All Transports

The transporting officer must always restrain prisoners (with handcuffs, "belly chains," or "waistraints") during transports, except
- In detention cells.
- In courtrooms.
- On aircraft when airline rules prohibit them.

[*] *paragraph revised*

(This Page for Notes)

Chapter Five:

PROCEDURES

How to plan and write a procedure in playscript.

After deciding to write a procedure, you may attempt to begin writing too soon. And the better you know your subject, the stronger you'll feel that urge to "get started." But procedure writing requires the same first step as policy writing: clear thinking.

A procedure, as defined in Chapter Three, "lists in order the steps a team takes to complete an action loop." It shows the team which member does what and when to do it. Part One of this chapter explains how to use that definition to think through a procedure. You'll learn how to use another thinking tool, the *Procedure Planner*. (Use the blank *Planner* in your Writer's Kit as a master for making copies.)

Like Chapter Four, this chapter focuses first on planning, then on writing.

Part Two builds on that thinking base and moves through the writing stage, describing how to use the *Procedure Layout and Writing Guide*, also in your Writer's Kit.

On the surface, the procedures you will learn to write in this chapter differ greatly from the policies in Chapter Four. But underneath, the reader's needs will still guide your writing. Policies meet the reader's need to know the rules. Procedures meet the reader's need for a map through the complex maze of team action. To do that effectively, procedures require a format unlike the layout for policies.

Part One: Planning a Procedure

Follow these six steps as you use a copy of the *Procedure Planner*. Each step is explained in the following pages.

1. *Write a title in which the first word ends in "-ing."*

2. *Define the "trigger" and "target" of the action loop (including the titles of those who start and end the loop).*

3. *Trace the steps from trigger to target using present-tense verbs.*

4. *Assign responsibility for each action, using the title of the person who will carry it out.*

5. *If special conditions apply, note these with the step.*

6. *Number the steps chronologically.*

To make all this practical, we will follow these steps to think through "Transporting Persons in Custody," the piece you first saw in Chapter One. In Chapter Four we sifted out the *policy* to isolate it from the other types of written direction. Now we'll screen the material again to identify *procedure.*

Before we begin, you may want to refer to the original version in Chapter One.

1. Write a title in which the first word ends in "-ing."

Complete your *Procedure Planner* with a pencil—one with a good eraser.

The first word in each procedure title should end in "-ing" Such a word will define the action loop and distinguish it from other loops.

"Transporting Persons in Custody," gets off to a good start. When readers see "transporting," they'll know the loop will not include such loops as "scheduling" prisoners for hearings or "assigning" them to cells. But the rest of the title, " . . . Persons in Custody," lacks precision. That's broad enough to include driving a prisoner to a dentist—a procedure that would probably not include the Deputy Compact Administrator. Let's revise it to read:

Title: *Transporting Probation and Parole Violators*

Now our action loop is small enough to deal with effectively.

Our title also happens to be identical to the one we used for the policy. Two questions may come to mind: (1) Are identical titles necessary? and (2) Are identical titles confusing? On the first question, no. The title for a procedure and its parent policy may differ. On the second question, no again. If the procedure title is the same as the policy title, the reader may still distinguish them by their differing numbers. Naturally, though, if you have two or more procedures working under one parent policy, each procedure will need a unique title.

Compare the following original titles with the rewritten versions just below each one. If you were searching through an index, which would give you more help?

Notice how the action loop comes into focus when the first word of the title ends with "ing."

(original)	**Public Disclosure**
(revision)	**Releasing History of Defendant**
	(suggests a well-defined action loop)

(original)	**Presentence Report**
(revision)	**Preparing Presentence Reports**
	(in contrast with "Distributing the Presentence Report," which is another loop)

(original)	**Bookings**
(revision)	**Recording Bookings**
	(says exactly what the team does with bookings)

2. **Define the "trigger" and "target" of the action loop (including the titles of those who start and end the loop).**

Think of an "action loop" as the sequence of steps needed to get something done. The action begins with a "trigger," which provides a clear starting signal to the person who takes the first step. The "target" of the loop must send an equally clear signal that the team has completed the work in this action loop.

Good example: A *shipping* loop might begin when a customer order (the trigger) enters the computer. The loop would end when the freight company picks up the order (the target). Notice that the trigger and target are distinct, observable events. No team member needs to guess whether they have occurred.

The target step of one loop can trigger the next loop.

Notice, too, that the target of an earlier loop may well serve as the trigger for your current loop. For example, a *taking orders* loop may end (hit its target) when the order enters the computer. But that same event becomes the trigger for the *shipping* loop.

Bad example: A procedure on serving warrants began with the Booking Officer *verifying* a warrant by calling a municipal court. Here's the problem: the trigger for the loop isn't clear—nothing tells the Booking Officer *when* to do the verifying. Every Monday morning at 9 a.m.? Within 24 hours after receiving the copy of the warrant? Or when?

That same warrants procedure ended with the Jail Release Unit *setting* an arraignment date. But the real target of an action loop on serving warrants is probably serving the warrant on the prisoner—or perhaps completing the paperwork that follows that action.

Now back to our example on transporting violators. As originally written, it did not identify the action that begins the loop or the person responsible for taking that action. But reading between the lines in the second paragraph suggests this action loop starts when someone on the team gets an order to transport a violator. Who is this someone? It looks as if the Deputy Compact Administrator receives the order—perhaps from the Parole Board—and sets the teamwork in motion.

So we could define the trigger in either of two ways:

Trigger: <u>*Parole Board*</u> **does this** <u>*orders prisoner transport*</u>

or

Trigger: <u>*Dep. Comp. Admin.*</u> **does this** <u>*receives order for transport*</u>

In the completed example of the *Procedure Planner* on page 5-14, you'll notice we have used the second of these two options.

Next, what is the "target," the action that ends the loop? The original version doesn't say. But logic tells us that the last step in this procedure must be delivering the prisoner to the chosen destination. Who is responsible for that last step? That would be the Transporting Officer. So the target line of the *Planner* would look like this:

Target: <u>*Transporting Officer*</u> **does this** <u>*delivers prisoner to destination*</u>

Notice that target—"delivering"—may also trigger a new action loop—perhaps the "admitting" loop.

3. Trace the steps from trigger to target using present-tense verbs.

(In actual practice you'll work out steps 3 through 5 together. But for now, we'll consider them separately for clarity.)

Use present-tense verbs to describe the steps in the briefest, clearest way.

Under the column headed "Verb" on your *Procedure Planner*, you'll be listing several action verbs. Each verb describes the next step one of the team members will take in the process of getting to the target.

At this point, the English language gives you a choice. Some people prefer to use directive verbs—the kind used in issuing orders: *Sailor, paint that railing. Son, mow the lawn. Driver, stop here.* In every case, an implied "you" comes between the subject and the verb: *Sailor, [you] paint that railing. Son, [you] mow the lawn. Driver, [you] stop here.* Writing with verbs that take the implied "you" is writing in the second person.

When we speak, our tone of voice can "tame" these second-person command verbs to sound quite friendly. In writing, though, we run the risk of them sounding harsh and demanding. To avoid that, many prefer to write procedures in the third person: *The sailor paints that railing. Our son mows the lawn. The driver stops here.* Third-person verbs usually end in "s," as these examples show. Now, instead of a command, each is simply a statement. The tone is now matter-of-fact instead of do-it-or-else.

If you write in second person, the steps will *command* the action. If you write in third person, the steps will *state* the action.

Leslie Matthies, who developed the Playscript method for writing procedures wrote: "Most people . . . prefer the third person; I do, too. However, the choice of using second or third person verbs is yours. Just be consistent." Following his advice, the examples in this book will appear consistently with third-person verbs.

As you write a procedure, think through the verbs that

describe the main action steps. Here are some of the verbs commonly used in playscript procedures:

telephones	**faxes**	**prepares**	**asks**
informs	**sets**	**requests**	**checks**
reports	**approves**	**decides**	**maintains**
returns	**sends**	**forwards**	**reviews**
obtains	**mails**	**installs**	**supplies**
distributes	**notifies**	**denies**	**transfers**

The verb, of course, can't stand alone. It will need support from a few more words that describe the action.   For example, in a step that reads, "[Supervisor] Reviews the overtime estimate for the next month," the last seven words describe the reviewing action. So under the column headed "Description of Action," you would write: *the overtime estimate for the next month.*

4. Assign responsibility for each action, using the title of the person who will carry it out.

Each present-tense verb will need a subject. In a playscript procedure, the subject will always be the title of the person responsible for the action stated in the verb. So under the "Title of Doer" column, write the titles of the persons who will carry out the actions described in the verb column.

Use working titles, not names. Names come and go as people move on. Titles change less often.

The *titles*, not the names. Sooner or later, many of the people in any team will move up, transfer, retire, or quit. When they do, they'll take their names with them. But they'll leave their titles behind. So use their titles, and you'll need fewer revisions.

The original written directions for transporting violators seems to have three titles in the action loop: The Deputy Compact Administrator, the Supervisor, and the Transporting Officer. Working as a team, they move the violator from point A to point B.

Normally the team members in your procedures will be part of your organization. They're the people who will read your manual. But now and then you may need to use the title of an outsider to open or close the action loop. For example, in a procedure on making photocopies for inmates, an inmate (not an employee of the prison) may well trigger the team by requesting a copy. That same inmate may appear in the target step as the doer who picks up the photocopies. In such cases, the outsider (non-team member) clarifies the beginning and ending of the action loop.

TIPS. Keep these tips in mind as you pencil into your *Planner* the titles of the doers:

- Don't repeat the title if the doer remains the same as for the previous action step. The doer most recently identified continues to be responsible for the actions in the verb column until another doer appears. In the wrong-right examples below, the Deputy Compact Administrator is responsible for the first three steps.

WRONG		RIGHT	
Dep. Comp. Admin.	1.	Dep. Comp. Admin.	1.
Dep. Comp. Admin.	2.		2.
Dep. Comp. Admin.	3.		3.
Supervisor	4.	Supervisor	4.

If the action passes to one or more other doers and then returns to a doer identified earlier, go ahead and repeat the doer's title as needed.

RIGHT	
Dep. Comp. Admin.	1.
	2.
	3.
Supervisor	4.
	5.
Dep. Comp. Admin.	6.

- Always include a "hand-off" verb between doers. In other words, make sure the last action of the earlier doer hands off the action to the next doer. In this next example, the hand-off verb appears in step three as the action passes from the Deputy Compact Administrator to the Supervisor.

Dep. Comp. Admin.	1.	Receives	Parole Board order for prisoner transport
	2.	Obtains	legal authorization for transport
	3.	Sends	written instructions & legal papers to supervisor
Supervisor	4.	Assigns	transporting officer

"Hand-off" verb

Think of the "hand-off" as passing the baton to the next runner in a relay race.

- Let the "hand-off" verb imply that the next doer has received whatever the action is. Example: If the quarterback passes [the "hand-off"] the football to the wide receiver, assume the receiver caught the ball. Saying something like, "Wide receiver catches pass" would add needless length to the procedure.

5. If special conditions apply, note these with the step.

Writing the next step in a procedure usually comes as naturally as the next step in walking. But not all action loops are that simple. Sometimes the doer must choose whether to go on, wait for something else to happen, skip forward or backward, or perhaps act before a certain deadline—depending on conditions at the time. These conditions generally fall into three categories:

Special conditions make the playscript format flex to fit conditions in real life.

- *Decisions.* On the basis of a condition you describe, the doer will decide how to proceed.

- *Simultaneous Actions.* Instead of just one doer acting, two or more team members will act at the same time (often independently).

- *Time Limits.* The doer will act in keeping with a time constraint you include (before, after, while, etc.).

Taken together, these can be called "special conditions"—special because they require choices or special attention. Let's look at each separately.

Decisions.

If-Then...

IF-THEN is the special condition you'll use most often. It tells the reader to do something only if a certain condition exists—and to skip the step if it does not.

For example, as you trace the action in our original example, you reach the point where the supervisor must assign the transporting officer. Normally, any available officer could do the job. But suppose the prisoner has a history of violent outbursts. Under those conditions, the supervisor should assign a seasoned grizzly bear! Did you sense the IF-THEN structure built into that situation? IF the prisoner has a history of violence, THEN assign a strong, experienced officer to the transport.

Your *Procedure Planner* makes it easy to set out an if-then step. You'll write the special IF condition in the *shaded area* just above the space provided for the verb and its description of the action. In that shaded area, describe the special condition in a statement that begins with "If." Like this:

If prisoner has a history of violence,	

Next, insert the verb and description of action as you would in any other action step:

If prisoner has a history of violence,	
assigns	experienced, physically strong officer

Other kinds of special conditions fit into the *Planner* in the same way. Simply write out the special condition in the shaded area and then link it to the verb and the description of the action.

When-Then...

Another special condition arises when the doer must wait for a specific signal to act. WHEN-THEN conditions may serve as triggers, but they may also be used inside a series of procedure steps.

The WHEN tells the reader, "Proceed only after this happens—and not until it does." Compare this with the IF condition which says, "Skip this step unless this special condition is true." So IF allows the action to continue whether or not a certain condition is true. But WHEN stops the action until the condition occurs.

Consider our transporting prisoners example again. An *alternative trigger* to the one shown in the example on page 5-14 might appear like this in the shaded area of your *Planner:*

		When the Parole Board requests a prisoner transport,	
Dep. Comp. Admin.	1.	Obtains	written instructions and any legal documents

Simultaneous Actions

Another kind of special condition occurs when two or more team members have to act at once. Readers read one step after another. Unless you say otherwise, they will assume the steps are done the same way, one immediately following the other.

But when actions happen simultaneously, the "hand-off" from one doer to another isn't quite as clear. Now more than one doer advances the action. You can help your readers follow the action in these cases by using such phrases as "*While,*" "*In the meantime,*" or "*At the same time,*" to get their attention and help them notice that more than one doer should be acting at once.

In the following example, the supervisor has handed the action on to the transporting officer. But as the transporting officer gets moving, the supervisor completes some paperwork:

Supervisor	3.	provides	officer with instructions, legal documents
		In the meantime,	
	3a.	completes	Form #1023, Report of Transp. Assignment

Time Limits

Time limits are another common special condition. Use these to tell a doer to start or complete (or perhaps repeat) an action before a stated deadline. As with other special conditions, include time limits in the shaded area of the planner. Here are some examples of how time limits might be worded:

Every 12 hours during the transport,	
telephones	Deputy Comp. Admin. with an update

Before the recreation period ends,	
verifies	the roll call

Within 30 days,	
files	copy of the completed transport report

6. Number the steps chronologically.

You're nearly finished with your *Procedure Planner*, but there's one more important planning step—deciding the order in which the steps will appear. Action loops happen in chronological order, so your reader will find that order the easiest to follow. The spaces under the # sign give you an opportunity to assign—and then revise if necessary—the sequence for your steps and special conditions. Suppose, after you've written the words, you discover that the sixth action will actually occur before the fifth. You can easily reverse them by erasing and renumbering.

One famous comedy show had an episode in which two characters had to disarm a bomb using a procedure that began this way:

Turn the locking screw on top of the bomb clockwise to the left.

But first, be sure to cut the yellow wire leading to the firing mechanism.

It's funny on TV—but not in the workplace. By using the *Procedure Planner* to stay strictly with the order of occurrence, you'll write directions readers can follow logically and chronologically.

Use plain-vanilla, Arabic numerals. Roman numerals may seem more impressive, but they're harder to read. You can always count on "6" coming across as six. But to a work-weary reader, VI may look a lot like IV.

Here are some principles to keep in mind as you decide on sequence and number the steps:

Trigger Step. This will always be Step #1.

Substeps. Often a special condition is simply a substep of a major step. For example, the special condition for transporting a violence-prone prisoner is really just a special condition of the "assigns a transporting officer" step. So you would sub-number the IF step as follows:

4.		
	assigns	transporting officer
	If prisoner has a history of violence,	
4a.	assigns	experienced, physically strong officer

Skips and Returns and Exits. A "skip" is a step that tells the reader to pass over one or more steps that follow. A "return" step sends the reader back to repeat an earlier step. An "exit" ends the action loop at that point—and may refer the doer to another procedure or to a task. Always number the skips, returns, and exits so they become sub-steps of the main action step they modify.

A "skip" example:

3.		
	submits	the report to District Court
	If the report was submitted earlier,	
3a.	skips	to step #7

A "return" example:

9.		
	verifies	form for complete information
	If form is not complete,	
9a.	returns	to Step #4

An "exit" example:

5.		
	locates	visitor's name on approved list
	If name does not appear in the list,	
5a.	follows	Task #415, Adding Visitors to Appr. List

Never repeat a number in the same procedure. No matter how many actors, number all the steps as a single series of numbers. It's one action loop, so it's one series of numbered steps. When the action shifts to another doer just continue the number sequence already started. The numbers follow the *team's* action—not the individual's.

You can still make changes after the planner is "done." Always think of the planner as scratch paper you can revise, add to, or delete from. It's merely a thinking tool—so once you've written some words, don't let them lock you in. Change them as needed.

The sample planner on page 68 is based on the original version of the transporting prisoners example. Study it carefully and see how each of the eight steps for planning procedures has been applied.

Summary: Planning a Procedure

- Your *Procedure Planner* (p. 112) will lead you through a thinking process that will prepare you to write.

- Identify a clear trigger and target.

- Lead team members from the trigger to the target with a chronological path of action steps.

- Assign responsibility by using the title of the team member who will take each step.

- Include a "hand-off" step each time the action shifts.

- Note any special conditions in the shaded area above the space for the action step.

- Number steps—and special conditions— chronologically.

PROCEDURE PLANNER

Title: _Transporting Probation and Parole Violators_
(first word should end in "-ing")

Trigger: _Dep. Comp. Admin._   **does this** _Receives order for prisoner transport_
     (doer)   (verb)

Target: _Transporting Officer_   **does this** _Delivers prisoner to destination_
     (doer)   (verb)

TITLE OF DOER	#	Special Conditions (if any)	
		Verb	**Description of Action**
Dep. Comp. Admin.	1	Receives	Parole Board order for prisoner transport
	2	Obtains	legal authorization for transport
	3	Sends	written instructions & legal papers to supervisor
Supervisor	4	Assigns	transporting officer
		If prisoner likely to be violent,	
	4a	Assigns	strong, experienced officer to transport
	5	Gives	written instructions & legal papers to trans. officer
Transp. Officer	6	Transports	prisoner as directed

Part Two: Writing a Procedure

In Part One. you learned how to use a *Procedure Planner* to help you think through a procedure.   Here, in Part Two, you'll take the next step—writing that procedure so that everyone in your organization can (and will want to) read and follow it.

Given today's pressured readers, that's a tall order. But management expert, Leslie H. Matthies, found a way to write procedures that makes reading clear and nearly painless.

Leslie H. Matthies is the author of the book, *The New Playscript Procedure*.

Matthies noticed the common ground between the daily "dramas" in the work world and the plays performed on stage. Playwrights assign roles to doers (the actors and actresses). So do organizations. Plays take teamwork.   So do most of the chores accomplished on the job. With this in mind, Matthies began to write procedures in the format that has proved so successful for writing stage plays. He called the method "Playscript."

In the rest of this chapter, you'll learn how to convert the rough notes from your *Procedure Planner* into the playscript format. As you'll soon see, the *Planner* required you to arrange your notes in that format. So you're already well on your way toward the final draft.

Some of the steps for procedure writing echo those for writing policies (Chapter Four), so we'll touch on them only lightly here.   Refer to the *Procedure Layout and Writing Guide* (p. 113) if you need to review these guidelines.

1. **Use a standard header to provide clear and useful information at the top of each page.**

Chapter Four describes the elements of a useful heading for policies. Use the same heading elements for procedures, with one change: replace the word POLICY with PROCEDURE.

2. **Start each procedure on a new page.**

As with policies, if a procedure ends part of the way down a page, don't start another one in the space left over. Start the next procedure on a fresh page whether you use a manual or an on-line system.

3. Transfer your notes from the Procedure Planner to a new page laid out in the playscript format.

Use these dimensions for your procedures:

Stay with these basic dimensions. Other combinations of column widths will prove to be less readable.

- *Margins—one inch left and right.* This allows three-hole punching, whether the text is printed on a left-facing or right-facing page.

- *"Action by" column—two inches wide.* If an actor's title requires more than two inches, use two lines.

- *Gutter* (space between the "Action by" and "Action" columns)—*one-half inch.* The step numbers go here.

- *"Action" column—four inches wide.* These shorter lines reduce friction and make the procedure easier to read.

These widths add up to 8.5 inches—the width of a standard sheet of paper. The example on the next page shows the basic playscript layout, with a variety of the possible kinds of steps shown.

PRO-### TITLE IN ALL CAPITAL LETTERS

Action by:	*Action:*
Title of First Actor	1. **Action verb** and description of first action.
	2. If condition, **action verb** and description of second action.
Title of Second Actor	3. **Action verb** and description of third action.
	3a. Simultaneous substep condition, **action verb** and description of action.
Title of Third Actor -OR- Alternate Third Actor	4. **Action verb** and description of fourth action.
	4a. If substep condition, **action verb** and description of action.
	4b. If substep condition, **action verb** and description of action.
Title of Fourth Actor	5. **Action verb** and description of action that requires reference to another policy (POL-XXX).
	6. When condition, **action verb** and description of action.

Title of Fifth Actor	7. **Action verb** with description of action involving a list of three items:
	   • Item 1
	   • Item 2
	   • Item 3

|-------------- 2" ---------------| .5" |----------------------------- 4" -----------------------------|

Glance back at the example above and notice four things:

- The action verb in each step or substep is printed in boldface type so the reader can't miss it.

- The lines within any numbered action step are single-spaced.

- Double-spacing separates the numbered action steps.

- The sequence of numbers continues through the entire procedure. The numbers do not start over with each new doer.

4. Point readers to any other needed policies, procedures, and task outlines.

Step five in the layout illustration above shows how to position a cross-reference where it helps the reader most—right with the step that creates the need for the reference.

Think of a reference as being either "macro" or "micro." A *macro-reference* provides broad information not directly connected with a specific step in the procedure. Place macro-references in the "See Also" line of the header. By contrast, a *micro-reference* offers help directly related to a specific step in the procedure.

In this example, the writer makes it easy for the counselor to find the task outline that elaborates on how to interview violators:

Counselor   8.   **Completes** and **documents** the initial interview (TSK-221).

5. When a special condition will not occur routinely, indent it as a substep.

Some special conditions can take the reader off the "main highway" of the action loop. Like side streets with only occasional traffic, such steps can be set off from the main step sequence by indenting them.

When a special condition causes a detour, indent it to make it visible.

For example, consider these three steps from a procedure on arranging medical treatment for inmates:

Med. Coord.   2.   **Requires** the inmate to complete a medical request form.

3.   If medical attention is required, **signs** the form and **forwards** it to the Health Care Coordinator.

3a. If medical attention is not

required, **informs** the inmate and **files** the request in the inmate's record.

The IF-THEN condition in Step 3. is the normal condition—therefore, it belongs on the main highway of the action sequence. But the special condition in Step 3a. takes the reader down a road less traveled by. By indenting the substep, you signal the reader that this is a side street.

Notice that the step number is repeated with the substep. The step is "3a.," not just "a." Redundant? Not in playscript format. If a step with several substeps carries over onto the next page, this repeated number helps the reader relate it to the main step at once.

As shown in steps 3. and 3a. above, the special condition should precede the verb. This up-front position makes it highly visible, reducing the risk that the reader may miss seeing it.

Here's an example in which substep 4a. directs the Shift Supervisor to take simultaneous action even though the main action has been handed off to the Deck Officers:

Shift Supv. 3. **Orders** a general lockdown of all inmates.

4. **Orders** Deck Officers to conduct a name and number count of all inmates to determine who escaped.

    4a. During the inmate count, **notifies** these officials and agencies of the escape:
- County Police Department
- Jail Commander
- Dept. of Rehabilitative Services.

Yes, in playscript format you may indent even just one subordinate item.

In this example you probably noticed that step 4. only has one substep—there's a step "4a." but no "4b." Back in school, when you had to prepare Roman numeral outlines to survive English class, the teacher probably marked you down if you indented with only one subordinate element. But don't worry about that rule in playscript. If it takes only one substep to cover the thought, use only one. (Your English teacher will never know.)

6. Separate Doers with "-OR-" When More Than One May Act

Now and then you may need to allow more than one person to carry out a step. For example, suppose any of three persons may trigger the procedure. To show that in playscript format, list all three doers in the "Action By" column, but separate them with an -OR- between them. Like this:

Any Employee   1. **Learns** of a new state or federal
   -OR-   rule requiring a revised form.
Procedure Writer
   -OR-
Superintendent

In that same example, suppose the first step might also be the simple discovery that a new form should be devised. In that case, place the -OR- between the action steps. Repeat the step number and attach an alphabetic suffix to it. But don't indent, because either Step 1a or Step 1b is on the main line. Putting this all together, the example might look like this:

Any Employee   1a. **Learns** of a new state or federal
   -OR-   rule requiring a revised form.
Procedure Writer   -OR-
   -OR-   1b. **Identifies** a practical need for
Superintendent   revision of an existing form.

In this case, any of the three doers may take either of the alternative steps numbered 1.

By now, you're probably ready to give the procedure to a typist to get it out of your sight. First you planned it. Then you revised your plan. And now you've written it in playscript format. Isn't that enough? Not quite. Even professional writers admit there's no such thing as good writing—just good rewriting.

When you review your draft, first read the procedure through once—start to finish—to make sure the words would make sense to someone new to the game. Then review the draft again using these checksteps, which are also listed on the *Procedure Layout and Writing Guide* in your Writer's Kit (p. 113). *(The examples used to illustrate these checksteps came from material written by writers new to the playscript method.)*

You'll save time and work in the long run by reviewing your draft in light of these checksteps.

Checkstep 1. Does each doer's last step forward the action to the next doer?

Think of the action in a procedure as a football. It changes hands—sometimes several times—on its way to the goal. Your written procedure should make it clear how the action "football" gets from one hand to the next. In the following example, the reader would be hard-pressed to see how the action passes from the fiscal technician to the counselor:

Fiscal Technician   3. **Sets up** the inmate financial record.

   4. **Issues** the canteen card to the inmate.

Counselor   5. **Assigns** the inmate, with his personal property, to Duty Staff.

It's possible that the counselor acts first. If that's true, then the problem is one of sequence. Or it may be that the technician notifies the counselor. Or perhaps the technician needs to tell the inmate to report to the counselor. Whatever the problem, this example shows the importance of making it clear how the action passes from hand to hand.

Checkstep 2. Are the steps in parallel form?

If your steps fall out of parallel, they'll make it hard for the reader to follow.

Here are some examples. The revision that follows each original example shows how to put the action step back into parallel form. Notice that each verb in the revisions ends with an "s."

(original)	1.	Verbally **requests** permission ...
(revision)	1.	**Requests** permission ...
(original)	2.	Shall **decide** ...
(revision)	2.	**Decides** ...
(original)	3.	Will **complete** ...
(revision)	3.	**Completes** ...
(original)	4.	**Review** the form ...
(revision)	4.	**Reviews** the form ...

Checkstep 3. Does one person's action hide within the action of another?

Playscript spotlights each doer in the left column. Readers soon learn to scan the left column to find their steps quickly and easily. So be careful not to conceal a doer in the action column—like this:

Counselor	5.	**Gives** the form to the secretary to be placed on the approved list, or with instructions for further action.

"To be placed" conceals an action that belongs to the secretary. But the busy secretary might easily overlook this step because both the doer's title and the action verb are hiding inside a step for the counselor. Solution: Insert an extra step in which the secretary places the name on the approved list.

Checkstep 4. Does any action step conceal more than one action?

Just as the "Action By" column spotlights doers, the "Action" column calls attention to individual action steps.

In most cases, each major action verb needs the high visibility provided by a separate sequence number and step (or substep).

Each step should reveal, not conceal, action.

Consider this action step:

Inmate	2.	**Completes** a special visit request form, stating the reason for the request and

giving the form to the counselor at least 24 hours in advance of the requested visit.

This appears as one step—but it actually contains two distinct action steps, *completes* and *gives*, both of which need equal emphasis. Notice how much easier it is to see the key actions in this revision

Inmate   2. **Completes** a special visit request form, stating the reason for the request.

              3. At least 24 hours before the desired visit, **gives** the special visit request form to the counselor.

Exception: When all the actions have the same object, or when they all fit snugly into one brief step, you may choose to combine them. Two examples:

Supervisor   8. **Reviews**, **signs**, and **dates** the request form.

Escort   9. **Prepares** and **distributes** the approved visit list.

Checkstep 5. Does any step state the obvious?

Writing a procedure requires you to walk the narrow ledge between saying too much and too little. Too little information leaves your readers guessing what to do. Too much seems to call your readers' IQ into question and turns reading into drudgery. So when you write, picture yourself in your readers' roles. Tell them all what they need to know. But leave out everything else.

Here's an action step that says too much:

Secretary   3. **Completes** the form, showing the inmate's name, prisoner number, the date, counselor, and who he wishes to see (doctor, dentist, etc.).

The form itself will prompt the reader to fill in the names, numbers, and dates. The procedure simply tells who fills out the form and at what point in the sequence of steps.

Not giving the reader any credit for common sense is another way to say too much. This next example spells out far more than anyone needs to be told:

Supervisor   2. **Submits** the report to the typist.

Typist   3. **Types** the draft report.

             4. **Proofreads** and **corrects** the draft.

             5. **Makes** copy of corrected report.

             6. **Returns** copy to Supervisor.

Why not just assume the supervisor knows how to get a report into final form (and that typists know their part in this routine transaction)? Perhaps like this:

Supervisor   2. **Has** the report typed, proofread, and copied.

Checkstep 6.   Can you tighten the wording?

Once you have a procedure in draft form, check to see if any steps lead the reader through two miles of words to cover two-blocks of action. Look for unnecessary detail and repetitions. Here's part of a verbose procedure:

Clerk   2. **Enters** the following information on the information card:
                 • Defendant's computer control number
                 • Defendant's name
                 • Defendant's date of birth

The number, name, and birth date all belong to the defendant. So why not combine all this into one easy step:

Clerk   2. **Enters** the defendant's data on the information card:
                 • computer control number
                 • name
                 • date of birth

If the card itself will prompt the clerk to include these details, omit everything after the colon.

Avoid both overkill and incompleteness.

Checkstep 7. Are there enough words to convey the whole idea?

As you trim the fat from your draft, take care not to cut into the meat of the procedure. Go for brevity, but don't give up clarity to get it. In the next example, the reader comes up short of words—and may misread the meaning:

Cashier 　　　6. **Takes** $10.00 to the Court Cashier for receipt.

　　　　　　　7. **Takes** to data entry area.

The takes *what* to the data entry area? The ten dollars? The Court Cashier? Or the receipt? As you edit your procedure, let Checksteps 6 and 7 balance each other. Avoid both overkill and incompleteness.

Mixing policy into the playscript format makes a sluggish document out of one meant for high-speed reading and action.

Checkstep 8. Did you mix policy or tasks with the procedure?

Policies—management decisions—don't belong in the playscript format. If you find material that fits the definition of a policy, put it in the related policy statement where it belongs. The writer in the next example mixed policy and procedure:

Medical 　　　4. **Prioritizes** all medical/dental requests
Coordinator 　　　and makes the needed appointments. Medical appointments are on Tuesdays and Thursdays at 10 a.m. Exceptions are on an emergent basis only.

Someone decided that medical appointments could be made on only Tuesdays and Thursdays, and only at 10 a.m., and that exceptions would be permitted only in emergencies. All that should have been stated in a policy—not buried under words like "prioritizes" and "emergent basis" in an action step that may be read by just one person (the doer).

**General Rule:
If you've listed five or six steps without handing off the action to another doer, you've probably shifted into writing a task.**

It's harder to define the line between task and procedure. Here's a general rule: If a playscript procedure directs the same person to take five or six steps without passing the action along to another doer, you may have shifted your focus from team action (procedure) to individual action (task outline).

The action loop in the next example has to do with preparing a presentence report—an action that requires teamwork.   But notice what happens at step 6.

Receptionist   5. **Sends** the presentence report to the counselor.

Counselor   6. **Makes** an appointment for an interview.

7. **Orders** all the inmate's records: violator history, DMV records, and FBIU and SPD rapsheets.

8. **Interviews** the inmate.

9. **Contacts** the inmate's references, the victims, and any other individuals or agencies involved in the case.

10. **Makes** an assessment and sentencing recommendation.

11. **Writes** the assessment report.

12. At least six days before the hearing, **sends** the report to word processing.

Typist   13. **Types** and **returns** the report.

At step 6, the procedure shifts its focus from its wide-angle focus on team action and zooms in on individual action.

Is the information useful? Yes—to the Counselor. But why ask the other team members to read through seven steps they will never act on?   Instead, most of the action in steps 6 through 12 should be transferred into a task outline with a title like, "Researching the Presentence Report."

In the procedure, something like this would probably provide enough information for the team:

Receptionist   5. **Sends** the presentence report card to the counselor.

Counselor 6. **Researches** the case and
       writes the report (TSK-###).

        7. At least six days before the
        hearing, **sends** the report to word
        processing.

Typist   8. **Types** and **returns** the report.

Checkstep 9. Do the trigger and target define a true action loop?

Writers just learning playscript often begin with a trigger that fails to say when the first doer moves into action. And they often end with a target that leaves the procedure dangling with an unfinished loop. This writer managed to do both in a procedure called "Revising Written Direction."

It's not enough for first and last steps to *look* like triggers and targets, they must always do the work of triggers and targets.

Originator 1. **Marks** changes on document.

        2. **Prepares** transmittal form for word processing.

Typist   3. **Retrieves** appropriate diskette.

        4. **Makes** changes.

        5. **Proofreads** revised text.

        6. **Prints** final copy.

        7. **Routes** final copy to originator.

Originator 8. **Submits** final copy for approval.

This seems to mix in some word processing task—a problem we noted in Checkstep 8. But aside from that, notice how the trigger does not tell the Originator *when* to mark the change on a document. No doubt the Originator must first spot a problem with the existing document. So the first action step might read:

Originator   1. **Notices** a need to revise the document.

Step 8 looks like a target because it appears last in the sequence. But is it a logical last step? If the "final copy" still needs approval, the revising action still isn't quite over. As Step 8 stands, the team will have no way of knowing who should take that last step of final approval.

The next page pulls the material in this chapter together by showing a final draft of the procedure written for our running example on transporting probation and parole violators.

Effective Date:	**PROCEDURE**	Page: of
Cancels: See Also:		Approved by: _____

PRO-321A <u>TRANSPORTING PROBATION AND PAROLE VIOLATORS</u>

Action by:	*Action:*
Deputy Compact Administrator	1. **Receives** notice from the Parole Board to transport a probation or parole violator.
	2. **Obtains** legal authority to move the prisoner (TSK-321B).
	3. **Sends** written instructions and any required legal forms to the responsible supervisor.
Supervisor	4. **Assigns** a Transporting Officer (or Probation and Parole Officer) to transport the prisoner.
	4a. If the prisoner is likely to be violent, **assigns** an experienced, physically strong officer.
	5. **Gives** the transporting officer the written instructions and any legal forms required.
Transporting Officer	6. **Transports** the prisoner as directed (TSK-321A).

(This Page for Notes)

Chapter Six:

TASK OUTLINES

Action sequences for one in cookbook style

In many ways a task resembles a procedure. Each consists of a number of steps. Each occurs in chronological order. And each forms an action loop between a trigger and a target. As a result, the format that works best for writing out a task looks almost like the playscript format.

Almost like—but not exactly like. As you'll recall from the definitions in Chapter Three, a task differs from a procedure in one important way. The action steps in a procedure involve a team—two or more people. *But the action steps in a task direct the efforts of just one person.*

The format for a task outline differs from the playscript format in one important way.

That difference suggests a unique format for writing task outlines. Unlike procedures written in playscript format, task outlines do not require an "Action By" column on the left side. One person carries out all the action steps, so repeating the doer's title would be redundant. Task outlines in typical narrative style often bulge with that kind of useless repetition.

In the following example, notice how the "officer" and pronouns referring to the officer ("he" and "his") keep appearing again and again:

The prisoner should be asked to remove all the items in his pockets and to place them in his hat. If he is not wearing a hat, the items should be placed on a table at some distance from the spot where the frisk is to be conducted. The prisoner should stand with his feet apart and his arms extended from his sides. The officer should begin the search by running the prisoner's collar between his fingers, feeling for any hidden items such as wire, small hacksaw blades, paper, etc. He should then proceed downward, running his hands over the shoulders and down the arms to the shirt cuffs, up under the arms and under the armpits, and down the shirt front, checking the

pocket and ending up at the front of the prisoner at his beltline. The belt should be loose, and the <u>officer</u> should check the belt and trousers by running <u>his</u> hands around the prisoner's waist; <u>he</u> should then proceed down the buttocks to one leg. Both hands should be used to check each leg, and particular attention should be paid to the cuffs. After <u>he</u> has searched one leg, the <u>officer</u> should proceed to the other leg and the abdomen. The crotch should be checked at the time the legs and upper thighs are being searched.

Hard to read? No question about it. Part of the problem comes from the method this narrative paragraph uses to refer to the searcher. The method creates three difficulties.

First, the writer alternated between the words "officer" and "he," probably in an attempt to avoid repeating the same word. But this makes the piece wordy and so reduces the reader's incentive to plow through it.

Second, passive sentences make it hard to keep the officer in focus at all. For example, the piece begins: "The prisoner should be asked. . . ." Who will ask the prisoner? The narrative doesn't make that immediately clear.

Tasks read best when written in the cookbook format.

Third, the gender-specific pronouns don't fit if the searcher happens to be "she" instead of "he."

By rewriting that example in the format used in most cookbooks, we can avoid all three difficulties and create a piece of written direction anyone can read and follow easily. Here's how it might look in cookbook format:

When the intake process requires a frisk search with the prisoner fully clothed, the **<u>Officer</u>**:

1. **Asks** the prisoner to remove all items from pockets and to place them in hat or on a table.

2. **Directs** the prisoner to stand with feet apart and arms extended from sides.

3. **Runs** the prisoner's collar between fingers, feeling for any hidden items (wire, hacksaw blades, paper, etc.).

4. **Runs** hands over the prisoner's shoulders, down the

arms to the shirt cuffs, up under the arms to the arm-pits.

5. **Runs** hands down the shirt front, inside the pocket, down to the beltline.

6. **Tells** the prisoner to loosen the belt.

7. **Checks** the belt and trousers by running hands around the prisoner's waist.

8. **Checks** the buttocks and crotch areas, giving special attention to the front and back pockets.

9. **Runs** both hands down each leg, examining each cuff carefully.

10. If the prisoner acts or walks in ways that arouse suspicion, **searches** inside the shoes and socks.

11. **Examines** personal items placed earlier in the hat or on the table.

12. If there is no evidence of contraband or concealed weapons, **returns** personal items to the prisoner.

As with policies and procedures, plan carefully before attempting to write a task outline. To help you, your *Writer's Kit* includes a master copy of a *Task Outliner* (p. 114). If you need a step-by-step explanation of it, review the material in Chapter Five that explains the *Procedure Planner.* The two planning sheets are very nearly the same, except that the Task Outliner has no spaces for titles of doers.

Once you rough out the task on the outliner, put it into final form by following the steps listed on the *Task Outline Layout and Writing Guide.* Again, because this Guide so closely resembles the one for procedures, we won't repeat that discussion here. If you need to brush up on items not covered here, review Chapter Five.

But there is an important point on the *Task Outline Layout and Writing Guide* you haven't seen before—Point 4. It says:

Task triggers belong above Step 1 in a lead-in phrase.

4. Begin the task outline with a lead-in phrase that:

    (a) Gives the title of the person who will do the task, and

    (b) Tells that person clearly when to take the first action.

The "lead-in" phrase plays two important roles. Let's look at each of them.

The lead-in phrase identifies who takes the first step—and when.

First, the lead-in phrase tells who's responsible for the action steps. It displays the doer's title up front where no one should miss it easily.

Second, the lead-in phrase gives the responsible person the "go" signal for the entire series of steps. So in a task outline, the trigger comes even before the first action step. The lead-in phrase ends with a colon, not with a period. The colon signals readers that more will follow to complete the thought. Thus mentally prepared, they will "carry forward" the lead-in phrase and relate it to the action steps.

In the frisk search task outline, notice how you can read smoothly from the lead-in phrase to any step that follows— for example, step 11.

When the intake process requires a frisk search with the prisoner fully clothed, the <u>**Officer**</u>:

11. **Examines** personal items placed earlier in the hat or on the table, watching for cigarette or tobacco packages.

Build your lead-in phrase so that the title of the task-doer appears immediately before the colon. To make it stand out, underline the title and print it in boldface type. By placing the title in this position, you set the stage for a third-person, present-tense verb in each action step—the same as you used in the playscript format for procedures.

Next, make certain that the first part of the lead-in phrase tells the reader precisely *when* to undertake the action defined in the first step. In the frisk search example, the officer knows at a glance *when* to take Step 1—"When the intake process requires a frisk search."

Some task outlines don't make the *when* so clear. Observe how this one begins:

When initiating inmates' property files, the **Correctional Counselor:**

1. **Gets** an empty property folder from the Duty Staff backroom.

In that example, the lead-in statement assumes the reader knows when to open new property files for inmates. Some readers may know. Others won't. Something like this revision would work better:

When the prison receives a new inmate or when a resident inmate acquires new property, the **Correctional Counselor:**

1. **Gets** an empty property folder. . . .

2. etc.

The lead-in phrase now supplies two clear triggers. The arrival of a new inmate or new property tells the Counselor to go to work on this task outline. How would you improve the lead-in statement of the next example?

In infracting an inmate, the **Infracting Officer:**

1. **Observes** that an infraction has been committed.

2. **Writes** an infraction report.

3. etc.

The phrase, "In infracting an inmate," (aside from the jarring use of *infracting*), does not tell the officer when to write up the infraction report. The real trigger is in Step 1. What the officer observes triggers this task outline. Notice how clear the trigger becomes when lifted into the lead-in phrase:

Immediately after observing an infraction, any **Officer:**

1. **Writes** an infraction report.

2. etc.

Everything else in the cookbook format works just like playscript.

Once you've written the lead-in phrase, complete the *Task Outliner* just as you would a *Procedure Planner*—minus the "Action By" column. Move through the action steps in chronological order. Keep the steps parallel by ending each action verb with "s." Handle special conditions in playscript fashion. And be sure to end on the true target of the task outline—one that closes the action loop that flows out of your title and lead-in phrase.

With the outline in draft form, take some extra time to evaluate it by the checksteps in the *Task Outline Layout and Writing Guide* (p. 115).

The next page shows how the Task Outliner might be completed for our standard example on transporting probation and parole violators. Refer to Chapter One for another look at the original.

On the page following the completed *Task Outliner*, you'll find that same example carried into a final draft in keeping with the principles listed in the *Task Outline Layout and Writing Guide*.

TASK OUTLINER

Title of Task: Transporting Probation and Parole Violators
(first word should end in "-ing")

Doer: Transporting Officer
(title of task-doer)

Trigger: Gets transport assignment   **Target:** Files report of transport

Lead-In Phrase: After being assigned to transport a prisoner, the
Transporting officer:

#	VERB	DESCRIPTION OF ACTION
	SPECIAL CONDITIONS (IF ANY)	
1	Gets	written instructions from Dep. Comp. Admin.
2	Reviews	instructions
3	Plans	transport
4	Arranges	own travel
5	Presents	legal papers to out-of-state officials
	If legal problems cause delays,	
6a	May place	prisoner in temporary detention
	If security problems occur,	
6b	May phone	Dep. Comp. Admin. for advice
7	Uses	restraints during transport
8	Avoids	discussing outcome of case with prisoner
9	Keeps	conversation with prisoner pleasant to reduce anxiety
10	Delivers	prisoner to prearranged destination
11	Files	report of transport with Dep. Comp. Admin.

Effective Date:	**Page:** of
<div align="center">**TASK OUTLINE**</div>	
Cancels:	
See Also:	**Approved by:** _____

TSK-321 TRANSPORTING PROBATION AND PAROLE VIOLATORS

After being assigned by the supervisor to transport a prisoner, the **Transporting Officer:**

1. **Gets** written instructions and any legally required documents from the Deputy Compact Administrator.

2. **Reviews** instructions.

3. **Plans** the transport carefully to anticipate and avoid difficulties.

4. **Arranges** own travel to the prisoner pickup point.

5. **Presents** legal documents to out-of-state officials to obtain custody of prisoner.

6. If legal complications or potential security problems arise:

   6a. **May place** the prisoner in a detention facility or in restraints.

   6b. **May telephone** the Deputy Compact Administrator for advice or assistance.

7. **Uses** restraints at all times during transport (POL-321).

8. **Avoids** discussing with the prisoner the possible outcome of the case.

9. **Keeps** conversation with the prisoner as pleasant and relaxed as possible to avoid increasing the prisoner's anxiety.

10. **Delivers** the prisoner to the prearranged destination.

11. **Files** report of transport with the Deputy Compact Administrator.

Chapter Seven

NUMBERING SYSTEM

Helping readers grasp the A-B-Cs by the 1-2-3s

A credit union published a two-inch-thick manual of policies and procedures without any numbering system. No one used it—and no wonder! It took longer to find the directions than to finish the work.

Numbers help us locate everything from paint colors to post office boxes. And the best way to help readers find policies, procedures, and task outlines is to provide them with a well designed numbering system. Such numbers give directions to the directions.

Readers need directions to your written directions. A numbering system offers the best way to provide those directions.

How to Number Your Table of Contents

As you read this chapter, you may be in one of three positions:

A. You already have a policy-procedure manual with an existing numbering system that works well. If it's working, keep it. As you issue new (or revise old) written directions, consider using the headline, playscript, and cookbook formats presented in this book.

B. You have a manual with no numbering system or with one that creates more confusion than clarity. In this case, consider restructuring your manual according to the system suggested in this chapter.

C. You are starting from scratch. This is the ideal time to introduce a numbering system.

Whether you're in position B or C, you can create a usefully numbered table of contents by following four steps.

Step One: Label and List Services

Make it a team project to brainstorm all the services your organization offers.

Sit down with two or three others who know your organization from top to bottom. Together, brainstorm to develop a list of the services your organization provides. As Chapter Four pointed out, services are the benefits your organization provides. In a restaurant setting, *meals* benefit the diners, *payroll* benefits the employees, and *maintenance* benefits the building. Notice that meals, payroll, and maintenance are labels that describe the services provided. They do not describe the specific work activitie*s* done to provide those services.

At this stage, don't worry about the order in which the service labels appear. Just name them clearly and write them down. Here's a list of service labels from a prison:

Grievance Resolution	**Release and Transfer**
Records	**Staff Development**
Transportation	**Admissions**
Payroll	**Business and Fiscal**
Fire Safety	**Segregation**
Emergency Preparedness	**Classification & Housing**

Step Two: Categorize Services

Rearrange your service labels so that services related to each other are in the same group.

Now scan your list of service labels several times. Ask yourself which of them you should group together. Shuffle the service labels around until you have several groups you think logically belong together. Then write a super-label that describes each category of services. For example, you might locate several centralized services under the super-label, "Administration."

Step Three: Assign Numbers

By moving up in increments of 100, you will open 99 policy "slots" under each service label.

Beginning at the top of your list, write "100" just to the left of your first service label. (Do *not* number the category label above it.) Then write "200" to the left of the second service label. Move through the entire list, each time increasing the last number by an increment of one hundred. By doing this, you will open up space for 99 work activities (policy titles) within each service area—201, 202, 203, and so on all the way to 299.

Here's another idea: Add one or two "vacant" titles at the end of the group in each category. Then, if you need to add some unforeseen service labels in the future, your numbering system will absorb them easily.

The next example illustrates Steps Two and Three:

ADMINISTRATION

If you include one or two "vacant" labels in each major category, you can easily add other service labels later without disrupting your system.

100 — Business and Fiscal
200 — Training and Staff Development
300 — Records
400 — Payroll
500 — (Vacant)

OPERATIONS AND SAFETY

600 — Emergency Preparedness
700 — Transportation
800 — Fire Safety
900 — (Vacant)
1000 — (Vacant)

SECURITY AND DISCIPLINE

1100 — Admissions
1200 — Classification and Housing
1300 — (etc.)

Step Four: Add Activity Titles and Numbers

With this skeleton in place, you're now ready to flesh out your table of contents. Pause on each service label you've just numbered. Ask: What work activities must we do to provide this service? At this point, write policy titles (one or more) under each service label. Remember, the first word in a policy title ends with "-ing."

At this stage, you will add in—and number —titles for your policies, procedures, and task outlines.

For example, under the 1100 — Admissions service area, a prison might include three policies: Booking Prisoners, Searching New or Returning Inmates, and Retaining Personal Property.

Assign a unique number to each policy title. Take the number from among 99 available numbers within that service area. For example, since the Admissions service label carries the number 1100, each policy number under it will belong in the 1100 series—1101, 1102, 1103, and so on up to 1199.

Prefix the number with the letters POL- to show that this is a policy: POL-1101, POL-1102, POL-1103, etc.

Next, under each policy title, add the titles of any procedures, tasks, or both that flow out of that policy. Give them the same number as their "parent" policy. But prefix each procedure number with PRO- and each task outline number with TSK-.

If you have more than one procedure per policy, add an alphabetic suffix after the number—PRO-1101A, PRO-1101B, etc. Do the same if any policy requires more than one task—TSK-1101A, TSK-1101B, TSK-1101C, and so on.   It's okay to use the same suffixes (A, B, C, etc.) for both procedures and task outlines, because the prefix (PRO- or TSK-) will keep them distinct.

Every work activity will have a policy. There are always rules (even if currently unwritten) that reflect management decisions about every kind of work to be done. But a given policy may or may not have procedures and tasks related to it. These combinations are possible:

A policy may—or may not—have procedures and tasks associated with it.

- A policy with no procedure or task.
- A policy with procedure(s) and task(s).
- A policy with procedure(s) and no task.
- A policy with task(s) and no procedure.

Here's how a section in your finished table of contents might appear. (You would add your own page numbers.)

SECURITY AND DISCIPLINE

1100 — Admissions

POL-1101   Booking Prisoners
   PRO-1101   Recording Bookings
   TSK-1101A   Fingerprinting Arrestees
   TSK-1101B   Preparing Booking Records

POL-1102   Searching New or Returning Inmates
   PRO-1102   Destroying Contraband
   TSK-1102A   Conducting Frisk Searches
   TSK-1102B   Conducting Strip Searches

**TSK-1102C   Conducting Body Cavity
Searches**

1200 — Classification and Housing (etc.)

This arrangement of numbers combined with alphabetic prefixes and suffixes can help you create a system that's simple and easy to cross-reference. To make things even easier for the reader, place each "family" of written direction together in the manual. That is, the "parent" policy would be followed immediately by any "offspring" procedures and tasks shat share the same root number.

Consider using contrasting paper to further distinguish policy, procedure, and task pages.

Consider printing policies, procedures, and tasks on contrasting colors of paper. For example, policies on white, procedures on yellow, and task outlines on light green.

The policy, procedure, and task that follow illustrate this numbering system. The set covers rules and instructions for revising written guidance in a prison setting.

Effective Date: 2/1/96	Page 1 of 1
POLICY	
Cancels: New	
See Also: PRO-374A, TSK-374A	Approved by: _____

POL-374   REVISING THE POLICY-PROCEDURE MANUAL

1. Employees May Propose New or Revised Documents

All prison employees may propose the creation or revision of policies, procedures, and task outlines by following PRO-374A.

2. MRC Committee Will Evaluate All Proposals

The Manual Review Committee (MRC) will consist of the following members:
- Assistant Superintendent
- Manual Manager
- Public Information Officer

This committee will evaluate each proposal for a new or revised policy, procedure, or task outline. The Committee may reject, revise, or recommend the Superintendent's approval of any proposed draft.

<table>
<tr><td>Effective Date: 2/1/96</td><td>Page 1 of 1</td></tr>
</table>

PROCEDURE

Cancels: New
See Also: POL-374, TSK-374A   Approved by: _____

PRO-374A <u>REVISING THE POLICY-PROCEDURE MANUAL</u>

Action By:	*Action:*
Initiator	1. **Submits** a typed draft of the new or revised document to the immediate supervisor.
Supervisor	2. **Forwards** the draft through the chain of command to the Manual Review Committee.
Manual Review Committee	3. **Evaluates** the proposed draft.
	3a. If the proposal is not acceptable, **returns** it to the initiator with a written explanation.
	3b. If the proposal is acceptable, **marks** any suggested changes on draft and **forwards** it to the Manual Manager.
Manual Manager	4. **Rewrites** the draft into review form.
	5. **Gets** signature approvals from the heads of all departments affected by the proposed document.
	6. **Compiles** a draft incorporating any changes suggested by department heads.
signatures	7. **Forwards** modified draft and department-head to the Superintendent.
Superintendent	8. **Approves** or **disapproves** the proposed draft.
	8a. If approved, **signs**, **dates**, and **sends** approved document to the Manual Manager
	8b. If disapproved, **returns** draft to initiator.
Manual Manager	9. **Issues** and **distributes** approved document (TSK-374A).

Effective Date: 2/1/96	Page 1 of 1

TASK OUTLINE

Cancels: New
See Also: POL-374, PRO-374A   Approved by: _____

TSK-374A   <u>UPDATING POLICY-PROCEDURE MANUALS</u>

After receiving an approved policy, procedure, or task outline from the Superintendent, the **<u>Manual Manager</u>:**

1. **Sends** copies of the new document to:

   - All staff members who hold master copies of the policy-procedure manual.
   - All staff in units and sections affected by the document.

2. **Requires** recipients to complete and return Form #72 to indicate that they have received and reviewed the document and entered it into their manuals.

   2a. After 14 days, **contacts** any recipients who have not returned their completed Form #72.

3. **Maintains** a file showing the history of the document, including approval signatures of department heads.

Numbering System for an On-Line Manual

Are you designing an on-line numbering system? You may want to consider the model developed by the Administrative Services Department of Whatcom County, Washington.

Designed to work within an organizational intranet, a nine-character identifier includes two letters, six digits, and a final letter. This system offers several advantages. Each identifier:

- Is unique.

- May be used as a filename.

- Works as an HTML hot link for cross-referencing.

- Allows you to distinguish between documents that affect the entire organization (such as *administrative* policies, procedures and tasks) and those that apply only within a more limited scope (such as the *operational* policies, procedures and tasks of a department or division.)

The nine-character identifier reveals the following five types of information:

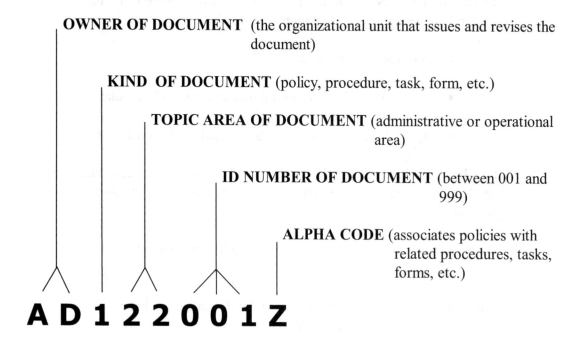

OWNER OF DOCUMENT (the organizational unit that issues and revises the document)

KIND OF DOCUMENT (policy, procedure, task, form, etc.)

TOPIC AREA OF DOCUMENT (administrative or operational area)

ID NUMBER OF DOCUMENT (between 001 and 999)

ALPHA CODE (associates policies with related procedures, tasks, forms, etc.)

A D 1 2 2 0 0 1 Z

Here's how Whatcom County assigns meaning to each section of the identifier:

A D 1 2 2 0 0 1 Z   **OWNER OF DOCUMENT (Selected Samples)**

Unit ID	Unit Name
AD	Administrative (Org.-wide)
A	Administraitve Services Dept.
AR	Assessor
AU	Auditor
CE	Cooperative Extension
CO	Council
	etc.

AD**1**22001Z   **KIND OF DOCUMENT**

ID #	Document Type	Alphabetic Abbrev.
1	Policy	POL
2	Procedure	PRO
3	Task	TSK
4	Form	FRM
5	Reference	REF

AD1**22**001Z   **TOPIC AREA OF DOCUMENT**

Numbers that indicate topic areas include both administrative and operations topics.

Administrative Topic Numbers: These range from 10 through 61. The following table shows selected samples:

	ADMINISTRATION	
10	Emergencies	
11	Government Operations	
12	Policy Management	
	FACILITIES	
18	Building/Property/Management	
19	Custodial Services	
20	Reserved for Future Use	
	FINANCIAL	
22	Asset Management	
23	Budget	
24	Cash Handling	
	etc.	

Operations Topic Numbers: In the Whatcom County system, the topic numbers 62 through 99 are reserved for Operations topics. These are "user-defined,' which means that those issuing documents at the Operations level decide how to use all 38 available numbers. Departments are not permitted to assign these numbers to any administrative categories.

A D 1 2 2 0 0 1 Z   ## ID NUMBER OF DOCUMENT

The three-digit format permits up to 999 policy document numbers in any topic area. Each policy can share its ID Number with up to 25 procedures or 25 tasks, as will be seen under the Alpha Code explanation.

A D 1 2 2 0 0 1 Z   ## ALPHA CODE

Every policy is tagged with a final alphabetic identifier, a "Z." For example, in the number AD122007Z, both the "1" and the "Z" identify the document as a policy.

As this "parent" policy spawns "offspring" (related procedures and tasks), each of those would carry the same ID Number, but with an Alpha Code in the range A – Y.

In the example above, suppose AD122007Z is a policy covering Accounting for Assets. The first procedure generated by that policy would be numbered AD222007A. To distinguish the second procedure generated by the same policy, the number would carry a different Alpha Code—AD222007B. And so on through Y.

The same letters would be used for tasks. The first task written for this policy would be numbered AD322007A. The second would be AD322007B. The third, AD322007C, and so on.

Chapter Eight

SYSTEM MANAGEMENT

Keeping your policy-procedure system in top shape

Guard your hard work with a well-designed system to manage the documents you've produced.

The earlier chapters of this book have discussed how to plan and write policies, procedures, and task outlines. An effective manual comes together only with top-rate planning and writing. But if all that effort is to pay off, you'll need to go one step further by making your system of written direction work within the unique context of your organization.

That's the point of this last chapter. We'll look at some techniques for getting the most value from your writing efforts. You won't find a full treatment here, because this book focuses on the planning and writing stages. For a more detailed discussion on these and related matters, see *Documents to Manage By*, by Leslie H. Matthies.

First, let's preview the areas we'll cover in this chapter:

1. *Getting the Most out of Your System of Written Direction.* Here we'll cover who writes and revises, the distribution process, training, publicity, and related topics.

2. *Whether to Write—and What to Write About.* This section will introduce a priority rater you can use as an aid in choosing the most pressing topics to write about.

Getting the Most out of Your System

Like a car, your system for issuing written direction needs a driver—someone to start it up, steer it around obstacles, and brake for stop signs. Unless one person takes responsibility for making the system work, it won't. And even if it does work for a short time, it will soon crash.

The person in charge of your system—its manager or coordinator, *must* have credibility in the eyes of everyone in your organization. So don't assign the task to some part-timer who reports to the clerk of the assistant to the deputy aide. Give the person a title that carries some authority: Policies and Procedures Manager, for example. And have your manager report to someone in top management who can make decisions that affect your entire organization.

Your system will suffer if its Manager doesn't have enough "clout."

With a capable manager in charge, you're ready to develop a system that can make a difference in the way your organization operates. Some suggestions follow.

1. Enlist working-level teams to draft content.

Two points here:

First, have *those nearest the work* develop the raw material that goes into any piece of written direction. Policy has to do with management decisions, so management should draft policy statements. Procedure and task? Find the people who must carry them out. Involve them in planning and preparing first drafts.

Don't expect your *subject* experts to be *writing* experts.

Second, appoint *teams* to do this initial work. Two or three people can think through a subject far better than one person working alone. A team may seem slow and frustrating at first because it will produce a wide range of ideas. But once sifted and refined, those ideas will give your written directions a depth that can come only from a multi-minded effort.

2. Have the System Manager write the final drafts.

Use copies of the various planners in the Writer's Kit to gather ideas from the people who will be affected by the written directions. Look to those employees for *content,* not for polished writing skills. Your Policies-Procedures Manager can bring the raw material into final form. This will promote a consistent style throughout, whether your written directions appear in a manual or on-line.

3. If you are using a manual, distribute master copies and working copies.

The sheer bulk of some manuals keeps them from being used as quick-reference tools. Pity the person whose ten-pound manual has to be split into two or even three loose-leaf notebooks because it has everything in it from buying lettuce to changing light bulbs.

Issue a few master copies and many field copies of your written direction.

You can solve the bulky book problem by issuing your manual two ways: in complete master copies and in abridged working copies. Into each master copy goes every policy, every procedure, and every task outline. Install at least one master copy in every large organizational unit (division, section, etc.). These master copies will serve as the policy-procedure "warehouses," storage sites for all your written directions.

But from day to day, most of your people will need access to only a small percentage of your written directions. So why not give each person a small "field manual," a set of written directions selected specifically to fit the work he or she does. For example, give your accountants just those policies, procedures, and task outlines that accounting work normally requires on a day-to-day basis. Be sure to include any other non-accounting directions the user might need to carry out each responsibility.

The field manual for supervisors should include all the procedures and tasks their people use.

Include in each tailored field manual the table of contents for the master copy. Make sure the list is labeled clearly so readers won't think their field copies are short of pages. Once they understand how to find the full set of written directions when needed, readers will appreciate having their easy-to-handle tailored versions.

4. Publicize your system of written direction.

Look for ways to make your system highly visible. Consider these ideas:

Babies have died from inattention. So have policy-procedure manuals.

- Post every new policy or procedure electronically or on bulletin boards.

- Every time you issue a major piece of written direction, print it in the employee newsletter. Accompany it with a short piece to introduce it and explain its importance.

- Prepare a special routing copy (an advance copy) of each new policy, procedure, or task outline. Make it hot pink, or some other can't-ignore-it color. Customize the routing list so that just the right people see it. Right after they've seen the routing copy, send them the permanent pages for insertion into their loose-leaf manuals.

5. Train employees in the care and use of your system.

Cracking open a new manual is no more fun than walking alone into a roomful of strangers.

Whether on paper on screen, your written directions ask for a reading—an activity many of us learned in school to resist. So it pays to walk your people through the material. Schedule periodic training sessions during staff meetings.

Although your training sessions will never make the Nielsen ratings, you can make them more interesting by observing a few simple guidelines:

- Stay away from the straight lecture presentation. Invite plenty of discussion. Use question-answer methods.

- For variety, try role-playing procedures now and then.

- Invite suggestions for improvement. Provide forms employees may use for recommending revisions or new pieces of written direction.

- Explain the *why* behind organizational policies. Have a representative from top management visit the training session to present the logic that resulted in this or that policy.

- Explain the rationale for any changes you make. When people know why something changed, they are more likely to accept the change and comply with it.

6. Define the revision process—and stick to it.

Everyone in your organization should know they're invited to suggest changes in the written directions—and should understand exactly what steps to take to do so. Revision is a work activity, so spell all that out in a set of policies, procedures, and tasks. Chapter Seven includes a set of written directions that demonstrate how one jail made the revision process clear in its system.

7. Purge and update your system regularly.

If you have an on-line system, this process can be carried out with the help of your information services staff. If you're using a paper manual, keeping the book up-to-date is more difficult. Ideally, every manual holder would keep his or her book current by inserting all new and revised pieces in their proper places and by throwing out the obsolete ones.

> **An out-of-date set of written directions get read little more than last week's newspaper.**

Ideally.

But in the real world, it's a good idea to call all manuals in for a periodic checkup—say every six months. During this "tune-up," the system Manager can make certain each manual has all the right parts in all the right places. It's also a good time to take inventory, to make certain all the books are still on the premises.

Whether to Write—and What to Write About

In writing direction—as in politics—it's all too easy to go to extremes. In a burst of enthusiasm, some organizations pump out more written directions than employees can possibly put to good use and more than the organization itself can maintain. In other organizations management refuses to commit any policies and procedures to paper, preferring the "flexibility" that forces people to work in the dark.

> **"Delegation cannot take place without definition—and definition requires documentation. So the cornerstone of any management system program is the effective documentation of the 80 to 85 percent of the activity that can be classified as routine and recurring."**
>
> *(From: "The Number One Management Problem," by Harold S. Hook)*

To the question "How many policies, procedures, and task outlines should we write?" there is no standard answer. You'll have to find your own answer by thinking through the documentation your organization needs. The following questions may help you through that thinking process:

- How many pieces of written direction can your organization maintain? Five? Five hundred? Issuing direction the first time is relatively easy. Keeping that direction up to date is more difficult.

- How much time can your system Manager devote to it?

- In what areas does the lack of written direction now cause problems for your organization? Don't write direction just to impress everyone with sheer bulk. Instead, write it to solve real problems.

- Which subjects generate the most questions and confusion whenever you add new people?

Once you've identified a number of must-write subjects, you'll need some way to decide which ones to write up first. Consider three areas as you assign priority to your writing projects:

- How *often* does the need for written direction arise?

- How *many* of your people should apply the written direction?

- How *urgent* is the need for written direction?

In your Writer's Kit, you'll find a *Priority Rating Scale* (p. 116) that includes all three areas in a simple formula. Use that page as a master copy. Distribute worksheets on which various people can tell you how they would rate a given topic. Combine and compare the ratings.

Assign your own scoring ranges. For example, a final rating of 1-9 might mean ignore this area. A rating in the 45-50 range might mean issue something here at once.

Summary

The suggestions in this chapter represent a great deal of work. But if your organization invests time, money, and effort in its written directions, it makes good sense to protect the investment. In short, here's how:

- Use teams of working people to gather raw material.

- Keep a consistent style by having your system Manager write the final drafts.

- Issue both "master" and "field" copies of your manual.

- Make your system visible through constant publicity.

- Train users how to use the material.

- Spell out how anyone can suggest improvements.

- Keep all parts of the system up to date.

WRITER'S KIT

Use the reproducible pages in this section to make worksheets to help you plan and write your written direction. You'll also find these worksheets useful for gathering ideas from those who carry out the work you'll be describing in your policies, procedures, and task outlines.

This section includes the following master copies:

Page

- **Policy Planner** 110

- **Policy Layout and Writing Guide** 111

- **Procedure Planner** 112

- **Procedure Layout and Writing Guide** 113

- **Task Outliner** 114

- **Task Outline Layout and Writing Guide** 115

- **Priority Rating Scale** 116

POLICY PLANNER

1. Write a title in six words or less that describes the activity and distinguishes it from other activities.

   _____

2. Describe the boundaries of this policy.

   _____
   _____

3. List your main points *(with any exceptions)*. **Management has decided**

   that _____
   _____
   (except when: _____
   _____)

   that _____
   _____
   (except when: _____
   _____)

   that _____
   _____
   (except when: _____
   _____)

   that _____
   _____
   (except when: _____
   _____)

   that _____
   _____
   (except when: _____
   _____)

   that _____
   _____
   (except when: _____
   _____)

4. Write the name or title of the person who will sign (or otherwise approve) this policy. _____

POLICY

LAYOUT and WRITING GUIDE

1. Use a standard header to provide clear and useful information at the top of each page.

2. Start each policy on a new page.

3. Write and rewrite the title until it describes the policy and separates it from others that may be similar.

4. Sum up management decisions in sentence headlines.

5. Make page layout work for your readers, not against them.

6. Limit paragraph length to 10 typed lines.

7. Limit average sentence length to 17 words or less.

8. Limit "long" words to 10 percent or less of your total word count.

9. Make at least 10 percent of your words work as active verbs.

10. Signal any revision with an asterisk keyed to a brief explanation at the bottom of the page.

CHECKSTEPS

❑ *Is this policy permanent?*

❑ *Will it relieve management from making similar decisions case by case?*

❑ *Is it a valid guide in more than 90 percent of all similar situations?*

❑ *Will applying the policy result in fair treatment for everyone involved?*

❑ *Does it fully convey what management has decided on this issue?*

❑ *Are any references missing?*

❑ *Did you cover all exceptions?*

PROCEDURE PLANNER

Title: _____

(first word should end in "-ing")

Trigger: _____ **does this** _____
                  (doer)   *(verb)*

Target: _____ **does this** _____
                  (doer)   *(verb)*

TITLE OF DOER	#	SPECIAL CONDITIONS (IF ANY)	
		VERB	DESCRIPTION OF ACTION

PROCEDURE

LAYOUT and WRITING GUIDE

CHECKSTEPS

1. Use a standard header to provide clear and useful information at the top of each page.

2. Start each procedure on a new page.

3. Transfer your notes from the Procedure Planner to a new page laid out in the playscript format.

4. Point readers to any other needed policies, procedures, and task outlines.

5. When a special condition will not occur routinely, indent it as a substep.

6. Separate doers with "-OR-" when more than one may act.

7. Signal any revision with an asterisk keyed to a brief explanation at the bottom of the page.

❑ *Does each doer's last step forward the action to the next doer?*

❑ *Are the steps in parallel form?*

❑ *Does one person's action hide within the action of another?*

❑ *Does any action step conceal more than one action?*

❑ *Does any step state the obvious?*

❑ *Can you tighten the wording?*

❑ *Are there enough words to convey the whole idea?*

❑ *Did you mix policy or tasks with the procedure?*

❑ *Do the trigger and target define a true action loop*

TASK OUTLINER

Title of Task: _____

(first word should end in "-ing")

Doer: _____

(title of task-doer)

Trigger: _____   **Target:** _____

Lead-In Phrase: _____

_____

#	SPECIAL CONDITIONS (IF ANY)	
	VERB	**DESCRIPTION OF ACTION**

TASK OUTLINE

LAYOUT and WRITING GUIDE

CHECKSTEPS

1. Use a standard header to provide clear and useful information at the top of each page.

2. Start each task outline on a new page.

3. Transfer your notes from the Task Outliner to a new page laid out in the cookbook format.

4. Begin the task outline with a lead-in phrase that: (a) Gives the title of the person who will do the task, and (b) Tells that person clearly when to take the first action.

5. Point readers to any other needed policies, procedures, and task outlines.

6. When a special condition will not occur routinely, indent it as a substep.

7. Separate doers with "-OR-" when more than one may act.

8. Signal any revision with an asterisk keyed to a brief explanation at the bottom of the page.

❑ *Are the action steps arranged in chronological order?*

❑ *Are the steps in parallel form?*

❑ *Will the person doing the task know exactly when to take the first step?*

❑ *Does any action step conceal more than one action?*

❑ *Does any step state the obvious?*

❑ *Can you tighten the wording?*

❑ *Are there enough words to convey the whole idea?*

❑ *Did you mix policy or procedure with the task?*

❑ *Do the trigger and target define a true action loop*

PRIORITY RATING SCALE
for
Policies, Procedures, and Task Outlines

Title (work activity): _____

1. How **often** does the need for written direction occur in this work activity?

1	2	3	4	5
Yearly	Twice Yearly	Monthly	Weekly	Daily

(Enter the number that roughly represents the frequency in Box A below.)

2. How **many** of our people will normally use written directions in this work activity?

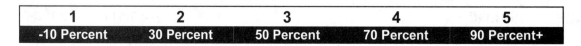

1	2	3	4	5
-10 Percent	30 Percent	50 Percent	70 Percent	90 Percent+

(Enter the approximate staff involvement rating number in Box B below.)

3. How **urgent** is the need for written direction in this work activity?

0	5	10	15	20	25
No Urgency					Critical

(Estimate the urgency and enter a rating number in Box D below.)

4. Calculate the priority rating by the following steps:

*   Step One: **Multiply** the number in Box A by that in Box B, and **enter** the product in Box C.

*   Step Two: **Add** the number in Box C to the number in Box D, and **enter** the sum in Box E.

A **B** **C** **D** **E** **PRIORITY**
☐ x ☐ = ☐ + ☐ = ☐ ← **RATING**

Ratings may range from 1 to 50. As you decide where the need for written direction is greatest, give priority to work activities with the highest ratings.

INDEX

Case, Upper/Lower 42-43

Color Coding 98

Cross-References 52, 72, 98

Definitions 23-30, 79

Headers 38-40, 69
— Approved By 39
— Cancels 39
— Effective Date 39
— Manual/Directory 40
— Page X of Y 39
— See Also 39, 72
— Signatures 35

Lines
— Length 17
— Spacing 71

Manual Management 103-109

— Manager 104
— Master Copies 104
— Publicity 105
— Revision 106
— Training 106
— Working Copies 104

Numbering System 93-101

Numerals, Arabic/Roman 65

On-Line Numbering 100

Paragraph Length 16, 43

Parallelism 17, 75, 90

Person, Second/Third 59

Policy 23-30, 31-53
— Activities 32, 41, 96
— Boundaries 32, 33
— Checksteps 50-52
— Defined 23
— Exceptions 34-35, 52

— Format 43, 53
— Layout and Writing Guide 113
— Management Decisions 23, 24, 32, 34, 41, 97
— Planner 112
— Scope Statements 33-34, 43
— Service Areas 32, 41, 94-95
— Subheadings 12-13, 42

Priority Rating Scale 118

Procedure 23-30
— Action Loops 23, 24, 25, 30, 57, 85
— Checksteps 75-82
— Columns 70-71
— Defined 23
— Format 71, 83
— Gutters 70
— Planner 114
— Layout and Writing Guide 115
— Special Conditions 62, 72, 90
— Steps
  — Action 76-77, 85, 88
  — Exit 67
  — Return 66
  — Numbering 65
  — Skip 66
  — Substeps 66, 72
— Targets 25, 30, 57, 81-82, 85, 90
— Triggers 25, 26, 30, 57, 74, 81, 85, 88-89

Readability Research 12, 44, 46

Revisions 40, 50, 106

Sentence Length 11, 44

Sequence 19, 26, 34

Table of Contents 40, 94, 98

Task Outline 23-30, 85
— Defined 23
— Format 86, 92
— Lead-In Phrases 88
— Outliner 116
— Layout and Writing Guide 117
— Pronouns, Gender-Specific 86

Titles 32-33, 56, 60, 96-97
— Prefixes 97-98
— Suffixes 97-98
— Vacant 95

Vague Modifiers 15

Verbs 41, 71
— Active 47-50
— Commonly Used 60
— Hand-Off 61-62, 75
— Passive 13, 47, 86
— Present Tense 59, 90

Word Length 12, 46

Writer's Kit, Worksheets 109-116

WRITING POLICIES AND PROCEDURES

FOR ALL WHO WRITE DIRECTIVES

Managers in many organizations have not found an effective way to direct staff action through the written word. Operations manuals—if they exist at all—are likely to be obsolete, incomplete, and nearly impossible to read.

This course was developed to meet such a need. It combines insights gained through:

- Twenty-five years of professional writing.
- Ten years of teaching writing for businesses and government agencies.
- Research into the most effective formats for writing directions.

Each class member receives a copy of the book, *Writing Policies, Procedures and Task Outlines.* The book includes master copies of planning worksheets that may be photocopied as needed.

After completing this workshop, participants have demonstrated ability to think through policies, procedures, and task outlines more effectively and to write them in words that make reading easy.

PROGRAM OUTLINE

1. Why Policy-Procedure Manuals Defy Reading
- How to recognize the 12 pitfalls of writing direction.
- Sources of "friction" that slow or stop readers.

2. The Three Main Types of Written Direction
- Policy defined.
- Procedure defined.
- Task defined.

3. How to Write a Policy in "Headline" Format
- Using the "Policy Planner" as a thinking guide.
- Ten steps toward writing readable policies.
- A simple way to identify revisions.
- Seven checksteps for revising draft policies.

4. Writing a Procedure in "Playscript" Format
- Using the "Procedure Planner."
- Handling exceptions.
- How to create the playscript layout.
- Nine checksteps for revising draft procedures.

5. Writing a Task in "Cookbook" Format
- Getting organized with the "Task Outliner."
- Tips on effective use of the cookbook format.
- Seven checksteps for improving task outlines.

6. Adopting a Workable Numbering System
- How to identify main categories for an operations manual.
- A numbering system without decimal points.

7. Practical Tips for Manual Writers
- Deciding whether and what to write.
- Deciding who should write.
- Maintaining the manual.

COMMENTS FROM CLASS MEMBERS

"Provides a clear, organized method for preparing written guidance and instruction for my staff . . . ."

"This is one of the most practical training courses I've ever taken. One I can apply immediately."

"If you need to write policies/procedures, it's the best available to date."

COURSE LENGTH: Two Days

CLEAR WRITING

FOR ALL WHO WRITE AT WORK

This workshop is designed to reduce the confusion caused by the poorly written word. Anyone who must write on the job (but is not a writing pro) will find the training both pleasant and helpful. Writing techniques apply to:

Letters	Memos	Reports
Manuals	Newsletters	Bulletins
Speeches	E-Mail	Minutes
	Proposals	

PROGRAM OUTLINE

1. Straight Thinking About Writing
- Resisting pressures that lead to gobbledygook.
- Job-related writing: art or craft?
- Visualizing your reader before you write.
- Check your writing motives.
- A realistic goal for on-the-job writing.

2. Organizing Ideas Quickly and Effectively
- Grasping the thought process for organizing
- ideas.
- How to decide what to include, omit.
- Choosing an effective idea sequence

3. Paragraphs that Give Ideas Away
- How to build the productive paragraph.
- Limiting paragraph length.
- Transitions—to keep your reader on track.
- The power of the well-written heading.

4. Compact Sentences
- What makes a sentence work in the reader's mind?
- Research results on sentence length.
- Four causes (and cures) of overfed sentences.

5. Right Words in Right Places
- Choosing words that get results.
- Common "word-focus" faults.
- The importance of word order in English.

6. Seeing Your Own Writing Objectively
- How to measure reading difficulty.

7. Punctuate to Prevent Confusion
- Specific answers to punctuation puzzlers.

8. Vigorous Verbs: Cut Fat, Add Force
- Four ways writers "kill" verbs.
- How to activate passive sentences.

COMMENTS FROM CLASS MEMBERS

"I expected the normal English composition course but was pleasantly surprised."

"Something everyone can use."

"This course is clear, concise, and packed with information. It provides basic information as well as practical application. It has been hailed as one of the best skill-building courses in our training program."

A COURSE YOU'LL REMEMBER

"Recall Boxes" make this workshop unique. These memory aids will help you visualize each writing principle by associating it with a simple picture. You'll receive a "Desktop Reminder" that displays all 17 Recall Boxes. With an occasional quick glance, you can review all the major writing principles covered during the two days of training.

Each class member receives the *Course Book for Clear Writing*. This loose-leaf book contains the text, examples, worksheets, and Recall Boxes. It's a reference tool you'll use for years.

COURSE LENGTH: Two Days

WRITING MINUTES AND MEETING NOTES

Those who read meeting notes often complain that minutes hide nuggets of action and decision inside pagefuls of wordy, often useless text. In this workshop participants learn how to condense meeting hours to minutes—written summaries that meet the needs of today's reader-in-a-rush

Topics will include: preparing to take notes, gathering and organizing the raw material, writing clearly and concisely, formatting the final draft, and indexing minutes for quick recovery. With guidance from the instructor, class members think through and create their own unique tools for these tasks.

Note: This course does not require any knowledge of shorthand or briefhand.

PROGRAM OUTLINE

1. Before the Meeting
- Identifying your readers.
- Defining the purpose of your meeting notes.
- Predicting what information your readers will need.
- How to design note-taking aids.

2. During the Meeting
- Boosting note-taking speed.
- The note-taker's proper role: Just seen? Or seen and heard?
- What about tape recorders?
- Handling digressions.
- How to participate and record. simultaneously.

3. After the Meeting
- Selecting final content: How to decide relevance.
- Choosing a sequence.
- Presenting material in a readable format.
- Verbal shortcuts for repetitive idea patterns.
- Increasing readability.
- Retrieving key information with easy-to-maintain indexes.

WORKBOOK INCLUDED

Each participant receives a copy of the *Course Book for Writing Minutes and Meeting Notes.* This book includes explanatory text, worksheets, sample formats, and examples.

COURSE LENGTH:
One Day